MODEL TRAINS

Series editor: Frédérique Crestin-Billet
Translated from the French by Susie Pickford
Design by Lélie Carnot
Copyediting and typsetting by Kate van den Boogert
Proofreading by Slade Smith
Color separation by Chesteroc Graphics
Originally published as La Folie des Trains Electriques
© Éditions Flammarion, 2002
English-language edition
© Éditions Flammarion, 2003
26, rue Racine
75006 Paris

03 04 05 4 3 2 1

FA1142-03-IX
ISBN: 2-0801-1142-6
Dépôt légal: 09/2003

Printed in France

Collectible

MODEL
TRAINS

David-Paul Gurney

Flammarion

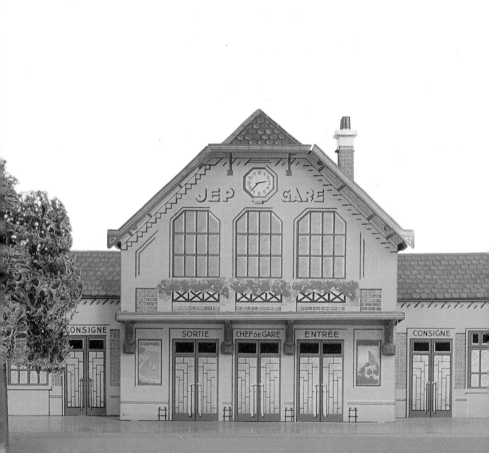

It was Fate—and a broken-down car— that led me to end up one evening in the small Swiss town of Saint Gall, sitting in the drafty old station that looked like the sort of charmingly rustic building you would expect to find in deepest Hungary. I immediately fell in love with the station and its quiet sense of restrained hustle and bustle. It was a cold day; everything was gray, and the soot pouring forth from the steam locomotives turned the air murky. I never looked back. From that moment on, I have never quite seen trains in the same light, and were it not for that evening in Saint Gall all those years ago, I would not be sitting here now in front of this page, as white as the fields around the town under the snow, soon to be criss-crossed by the sooty lines of my pen, like train tracks.

CONTENTS

Introduction

The year 1825 was a great moment in history, for it witnessed the opening of the first steam-hauled public railway, in England. This introduction to the fascinating world of model train collecting is not designed to be a serious history of the railroad, however; instead it aims to outline the key dates and developments in order to illustrate the rich history that lies behind the model trains we all treasured as children—and which many of us have never quite grown out of.

O f course, the principle of sliding a cart along rails had been known for a long time, but before James Watt discovered steam power in 1763, men had relied on horses to shift heavy loads. Watt's discovery sparked off the industrial revolution and encouraged inventors to try and devise a system that would harness this new source of energy. The first of these was the British engineer Richard Trevithick, who came up with a design in 1804 for a steam engine with enormous cogs and connecting rods powered by a boiler. The locomotive was born. Its earliest application was ferrying iron between mines in Pennydarren to Abercynon in Wales. Later, other engineers came up with improvements to Trevithick's design that resulted in a real locomotive that could be put to use transporting passengers. Two other British engineers, George Stephenson and his son Robert, were behind the designs for the steam locomotive, which they baptized the Rocket, which began "regular" service in 1825 on the Liverpool and Manchester Railway. At long last, in one of the carriages behind the locomotive belching steam, brave passengers could pay for a seat. In 1830, the first truly regular train service began operating between the two rapidly growing industrial centers, now major cities, of Liverpool and Manchester, with a top speed of 35 miles (55 km) per hour. This excessive speed was accused of making cows sterile and killing the crops in the fields.

An exceptional model Berliet railcar dating from the 1920s. This I scale toy was manufactured by Haman.

At the end of the 30s, Hornby developed very realistic large-scale electric trains, like this Bugatti railcar.

The rest of Europe soon caught up with this new technology, which, for the first time in history, meant that goods and passengers could be transported safely and reliably, with none of the risks and inconveniences of coach travel. France opened its first train line in 1827 at Andrézieux, near Saint-Etienne, for transporting coal, but the line was rapidly extended to the city of Lyon. The first German line opened in 1835, between Nuremberg and Fürth. The first international railroad, from Strasbourg to Basel, inaugurated in 1841, was also the longest

In this charming ad we see two favorite toys—Meccano, invented in 1901 by the great Frank Hornby (1863-1936), and the model train, produced by his company from 1920.

stretch of track ever attempted up to that date, nearly 90 miles (140 km) in length. America's first track was laid in 1830; Canada's, in 1836; Australia's in 1854; and by 1860 trains were in use in such far-flung corners of the world as Cuba (1837), Peru (1851), and Pakistan (1853).

By 1841, some 3070 miles (4912 km) of track had been laid throughout Europe, and almost as much in North America. However, it was not until 1870 that it became possible to travel from the East coast to the West entirely by train, while in China such a journey would only be possible in 1902, and in Australia in 1916. Perhaps the most impressive aspect of the history of the railroad is the way it sprang up so rapidly, expanding in a very few decades from Trevithick's early experiment with steam locomotion, to a fully-fledged, technologically advanced industry.

Stations, with their imaginary crowds of bustling travelers, were just as much a part of the fun as trains.

The expansion of the rail industry coincided with the rise of the golden era of nineteenth-century capitalism, and fortunes were won and lost by speculators rushing to invest in this new technological gold mine.

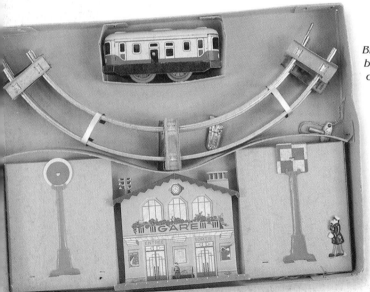

Brand new, still in its box: a simple clockwork train.

Paya, the pride of the Spanish toy industry, sold attractive model trains that were cheaper than their German rivals.

CATALOGO
FERROCARRILES
ELECTRICOS

MADE IN SPAIN

ESCALA 0

From the very beginning, people were fascinated, if a little scared, by trains. Children in particular loved the plumes of steam, the bright colors of the carriages, and the cheery, soot-covered stokers and engineers. Toy-makers were quick to take advantage of this, producing miniature versions of all these treasures for this new market, in factories that had only existed since the train had made the distribution of their products possible.

For generations, trains were a much-loved part of every little boy's childhood.

Although Hornby and JE. made fine trains, nobod. could beat Märklin in term of technical perfection

The first model trains, toys for children, were sold in general stores alongside bars of soap, pairs of shoes, and sacks of seed. They would be given pride of place in the window, and little boys would leave marks on the glass as they pressed their noses up against it for a closer look at the marvelous treasure that most of them could never hope to own. Peddlers traveling from village to village might also have a toy train or two in their wares, and hawkers would always be assured of selling a few at the local market. Most of the time, these models were cheap, gaudy, mass-produced toys in lithographed tinplate which had sharp edges that cut inquisitive little fingers. They would be given as a gift on special occasions such as a birthday, first communion, or as a reward

The magic of electric toy trains led many little boys to while away days on end playing at being stationmaster, with hours of innocent pleasure to be had blowing a whistle and waving a flag

Le Jouet de PariS

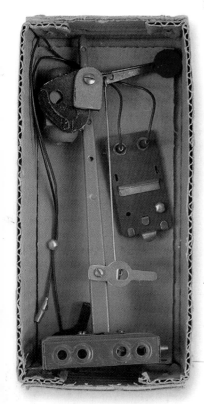

for good performance in school. As time passed, technology progressed, and people had more money to spend on their children, these cheap yet charming toys began to give way to more elaborate, more accurate models. The designs became more intricate, and the toy became a scale model that was almost too good to leave to the children. It was at this time that some of the best-known model train manufacturers started up in business,

uch as the German companies Märklin in 1859
nd Bing in 1863, France's CR in 1868, and the
panish company Paya in 1900. These and a
umber of other companies grew rapidly, adding

*Real, working points and signals taught children to run their trains.
Below, a fine example of the sort of colorful accessories produced
by Hornby to complete the illusion of a busy station.*

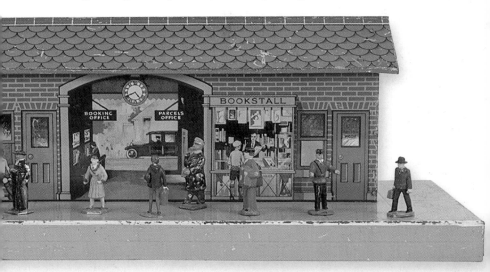

more and more sophisticated models to their ranges. By 1914, Märklin had 1,600 models in its catalog! Britain's Frank Hornby was a latecomer to the market, but his company underwent rapid expansion in 1915, when, for obvious reasons, importation of toys from Germany were suspended.

This highly detailed electric substation provided the low voltage needed to run the trains.

This sophisticated scener took several years t set up. It can be see at the Rambolitra museum in Rambouille south-west of Paris

From the most basic wind-up models to more elaborate electric engines or even models propelled by real steam power, model locomotives and cars are, for many collectors, real works of art—not to mention the painted stations, perfect to every detail; the working, electrically-operated signals; and the almost endless range of accessories to create the illusion of a miniature world. All over the world, people get together in

This Trans-Saharan express, running from Algiers to Timbuktoo, was the first model from the Jouef factory in France, founded in around 1950 by Georges Huard.

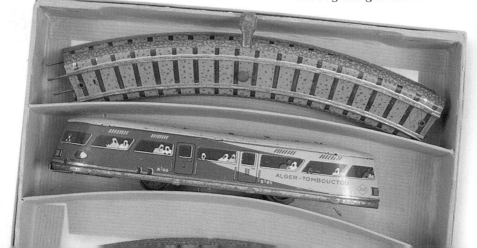

*A locomotive, one passenger car, two freight cars, and a set of rails forming
a circle. This gift, dating from the 1930s to the 1950s, would have made
a little boy very happy at Christmas.*

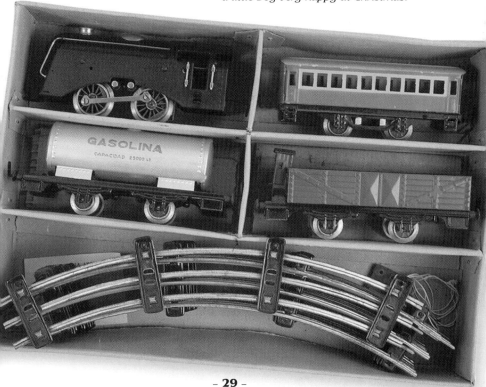

clubs to discuss the arcane delights of F units, HO gauge, and Irvington cars, eagerly scanning collectors' catalogs for the rare model needed to complete their collection; others simply fall under the charm of a battered nineteenth-century locomotive with an enormous key on one flank to wind it up, much loved by some child long since grown up, whose great-grandchildren now prefer to play video games than discover the delights of toy trains.

What sort of person collects model trains? Anybody and everybody: me, you—maybe the man across the street has a room entirely dedicated to his collection, who knows? For me, there are two sorts of collectors. There are those who collect trains for their beauty, and who are happy just to look at them. And then there are people

From the most basic toy made from old tin cans, to the superbly detailed network capable of running several trains at once, the world of the model train offers something for everyone—and it needn't be very expensive as the model on the left proves.

who spend all day at work itching to get home and play with their very own model railway. The most fortunate have a spare room, cellar, or garage devoted to their hobby, with several hundred yards of H0 gauge track. I used to know a man in Paris who bought all the cellars underneath his block of flats so he could build his own miniature world, with villages, rivers and lakes, tunnels through mountains, and with a capacity for up to twenty trains at once!

The collecting bug can strike in many different ways. Perhaps the most usual is to find an electric train under the Christmas tree, a present from a kindly uncle. This is how the Swiss collector Count Antonio Giansanti-Coluzzi began, and he ended up an acknowledged expert in model trains, with one of the biggest collections of trains of all scales and gauges in the world. Other collectors started simply because they happened to grow up along a busy train line, rocked to sleep in their cradle by the trains rushing past the house. My friend Guy started out like this. In 1965, he spent part of his first pay-check on a Jouef Railcar model.

Like locomotives and cars, model stations were not impervious to fashion. The model above is a fine example of the rather severe architectural style of the 1930s.

Now, over thirty-five years later, he is still working on his model railway, and gets just as much pleasure as ever from playing with his roughly 1,500 locomotives and cars.

You probably already know that there are thousands of other collectors out there, meeting in clubs, writing newsletters, exchanging models. Maybe you are a member, or even a founder, of such a club yourself. Whether you are a confirmed collector or a newcomer to the magic world of the model train, welcome to this big, friendly family—and happy collecting!

Gauges

If you are unfamiliar both with real trains and with model railroads, the question of the range of gauges available may come as rather a surprise. If trains were a recent invention, the various countries involved would probably have got together and agreed to work toward a standard size. But because trains were invented in the early nineteenth century that simply did not happen and a bewildering range of gauges were adopted in different countries across Europe and in America. In England and America, for example, the rails were 4 feet 8 ½ inches (1.44 m) apart, while in Spain, they were 5 ½ feet (1.68 m) apart and 5 feet (1.52 m) in Russia. In 1850, there was an attempt to introduce a metric gauge, but to this day, there are still fifteen or so different gauges in use throughout the world

or model trains (i.e., exact scale renditions of real
prototypes), gauge is measured between the two
outside rails, while for toy trains (which are not
necessarily to scale) gauge is measured from the
inside face of the two outside rails. The gauge is not
to be confused with the scale, although it is true
that the gauge is proportional to the dimensions
of the locomotive, tender, or car. A table showing
the most commonly found scales and gauges is
given on the following spead. The model trains
featured in this book are for the most part built for
gauge of 1.9 inch or
48 mm (corresponding
to scale I), 1.4 inch or
35 mm (0 scale), or
.65 inch or 16.5 mm
(H0 scale). H0 is
shorthand for half 0,
because the models
are built on a scale of
:87, half as big as 0
scale trains, which are
/48 real size.

Scales and Gauges

Scale	Date	Gauge	Approximate scale of reduction
IV	Prior to 1914	3" (75 mm)	-
III	Prior to 1914	3" (75 mm)	-
Standard	1906-30	2.9" (73 mm)	-
IIa	Prior to 1914	2.6" (67 mm)	-
II	Prior to 1914	2.1" (54 mm)	-
I	Prior to 1925	1.9" (48 mm)	-
0	1900-65	1.4" (35 mm)	-
00	1938-59	0.7" (16.5 mm)*	1/72
H0	1950-present	0.7" (16.5 mm)*	1/87
I	Current	1.8" (45 mm)*	1/32
0	Current	1.3" (32 mm)*	1/43

*measured from the
inside face of the two rails

Manufacturers
Bing
Märklin, Bing
Lionel
Schoenner
Märklin, Bing, Carette, Plank, Schoenner
Märklin, JEP
Most manufacturers
Märklin, Hornby
Most manufacturers
Most manufacturers
Most manufacturers

This table gives the most common scales and gauges, although there are other older scales such as 28 and 33 (named after their gauge in millimeters)—used prior to 1914 by manufacturers like JEP, CR, and FV—and more modern scales, such as TT, N, and Z, with gauges of $1/2$ inch (12 mm), $1/3$ inch (9 mm), and $1/4$ inch (6.5 mm), respectively.

A s every true train devotee knows, steam locomotives get their names from the number and placing of their wheels, starting from the front of the engine. For example, a locomotive with two axles on a bogie, then three powered axles, then a Bissel or other axle, is known as a 4-6-2. This particular number and placing of wheels belongs to Pacific locomotives. This page shows more examples.

Diesel and electric locomotives are also categorized according to the number and placement of the wheels, but use a letter of the alphabet to indicate the number of driving wheels. A corresponds to one axle, B to two, C to three, and so on. The carrying or non-powered axles are numbered.

 2-6-0, Mogul

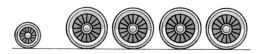 2-8-0, Consolidation

 4-4-0, American

   4-4-2, Atlantic

   4-6-0, Ten Wheeler

   4-8-2, Mountain

4-6-6-4, Challenger

Thus a 2D2 has two load-bearing axles followed by four driving axles, and then another two load-bearing axles. Where the wheels are gathered in groups on movable sub-chassis called bogies, each letter applies to one bogie. Thus a BB is a locomotive with two bogies, each with two powered axles, while a CC is a locomotive with two bogies, each with three powered axles. Note that the number of axles increases with the weight of the locomotive. Twenty-two short tons (20 metric tonnes) per axle is the norm, although this may be reduced in exceptional circumstances; for example, France's TGV is limited to 18.74 short tons (17 metric tonnes) per axle, to avoid placing too much strain on the rails at the very high speeds it reaches.

This Märklin model is a 1BB1 version of the famous 1CC1 Crocodile that operated on the

Swiss Saint Gotthard line. The original was made in 1920—this one is some ten years younger.

Many collectors are happy to spend a small fortune on models in pristine condition and still in their box. Will our grandchildren have the same thrill on finding an unopened video game?

I

model trains
LARGE-SCALE
LOCOMOTIVES

Forget the price for a moment. Shut your eyes and dream of your ideal train set. Will it be a Märklin, a JEP, or a Bing? These three companies were behind the twentieth century's most magnificent trains. Although they were originally made as toys, these locomotives are now seen by many collectors as genuine works of art, and are eagerly sought by enthusiasts the world over, who, if they are fortunate enough to acquire one, greatly treasure it. In the following pages you will find some of these noble creations, as well as others that, while less splendid and with less meticulous attention to detail, nonetheless have an indisputable charm. All of these locomotives are 0, I, or II scale.

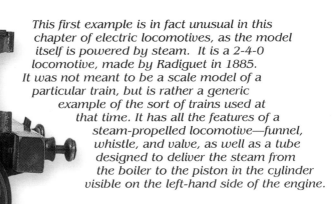

This first example is in fact unusual in this chapter of electric locomotives, as the model itself is powered by steam. It is a 2-4-0 locomotive, made by Radiguet in 1885. It was not meant to be a scale model of a particular train, but is rather a generic example of the sort of trains used at that time. It has all the features of a steam-propelled locomotive—funnel, whistle, and valve, as well as a tube designed to deliver the steam from the boiler to the piston in the cylinder visible on the left-hand side of the engine.

This simple train had no need for rails or sophisticated equipment; it was designed to be pulled across the floor of a child's playroom by a string attached to the front. The passengers, station, and scenery were as elaborate as the child's imagination could make them.

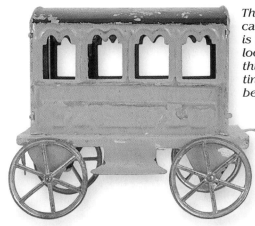

The scale of reduction of this car is not known exactly, but is in the region of 1/50. The locomotive on page 46 and this car are made of thin tinplate, and would have been used to transport miniature passengers made of lead. This car was manufactured by FV, who made models between 1864 and 1902.

*Pull-along trains were cheap toys that
could be purchased from peddlers and
market stalls. This example, with its
colorful pasenger cars, must have*

*...been the pride and joy of a little boy one
hundred years ago, as it dates from the
late nineteenth or early twentieth
century. Its manufacturer is unknown.*

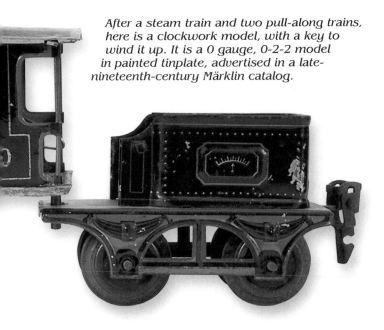

After a steam train and two pull-along trains, here is a clockwork model, with a key to wind it up. It is a 0 gauge, 0-2-2 model in painted tinplate, advertised in a late-nineteenth-century Märklin catalog.

A 0-4-0 locomotive and tender made by the German firm Märklin between 1880 and 1890. It is powered by a mechanical spring mechanism, which the child controlled with the levers that can be seen in the engineer's cab, at the back of the locomotive.

This 4-4-0 locomotive is rather a strange hybrid, with the shape of a British steam locomotive, and an American-style cab. It was made by Bing in the early twentieth century, and is powered by a mechanical driving system.

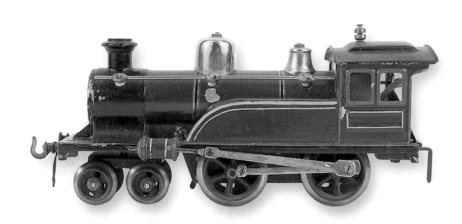

Another early twentieth-century example, but this Bing locomotive was powered by steam. Its whistle can be clearly seen above the boiler. The sound of the whistle, the noise of the steam being let off, and the smell of the burning alcohol boiling the water were an unforgettable delight for many little boys growing up in the early 1900s.

This Märklin locomotive, dating from the end of the nineteenth century, is not a model of a particular engine, but rather imitates the general style of trains of the period. It is a gauge I, 0-4-0 loco and tender with a clockwork mechanism.

This Bing clockwork model was based on the Wurtemberg Pacific, which had its funnel flared toward the front. It is a 0-4-0 model, and note that the gauge is written on the cabside in two ways: "O" and "35"; one being the name, the other the measurement.

*This early twentieth century model,
made by Märklin, is based on the George V
locomotive—its name is painted on the boiler.
It is an English 4-4-0, made in about 1910.*

This "Big C" 4-4-0 locomotive, with its distinctive "cow-puncher" front and its six-wheeled tender, was very fashionable in the early years of the twentieth century—both the toy version and the original. Beginning in 1898, a total of 120 of them were made, most in the livery of the French firm PLM (Paris-Lyon-Méditerranée) by Märklin. The gauge is 1.9 inch (48 mm), and the motor is electric. Note that "Big C" corresponds to the series C61 to 180, while the smaller "Little C" locomotives correspond to the series C1 to 60.

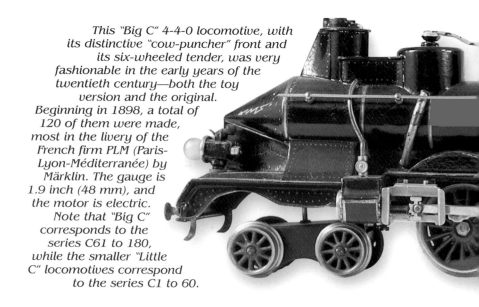

Here is another version of the "Big C" 4-4-0. Note the disproportion of the small wheels (1.9 inch, or 48 mm, gauge) in comparison with the size of the engine. The serial number CV 4020 on the cab is the maker's reference.

Clearly visible on the left-hand side of the engine is the enormous key that served to wind up the clockwork mechanism of this 0-4-0 locomotive with a twin-axle tender, produced by Märklin in the first decade of the 1900s. With the spring fully wound, a little train like this would run for about three minutes.

The London and North-Western Railway (LNWR) used tank locomotives similar to this on its suburban lines out of London in the early twentieth century. It is a 4-4-2, T gauge in hand-painted sheet steel, on sale in the Märklin catalog from 1910.

*This superb model, with a 1.9 inch (48 mm) gauge,
is based on an English 4-4-0 with a triple-axle
tender, and is powered by steam. The placement
of the wheels has been rather simplified, however.
It was produced by the German company Bing,
and was on sale from 1910. The letters LMS
stand for London, Midlands, and Scottish Railway.*

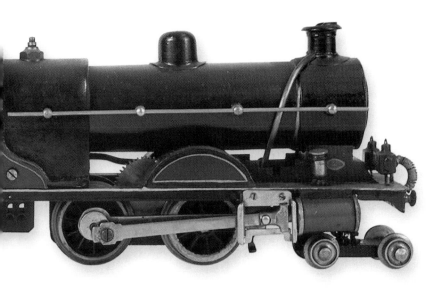

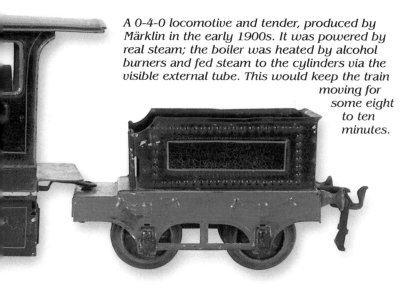

A 0-4-0 locomotive and tender, produced by Märklin in the early 1900s. It was powered by real steam; the boiler was heated by alcohol burners and fed steam to the cylinders via the visible external tube. This would keep the train moving for some eight to ten minutes.

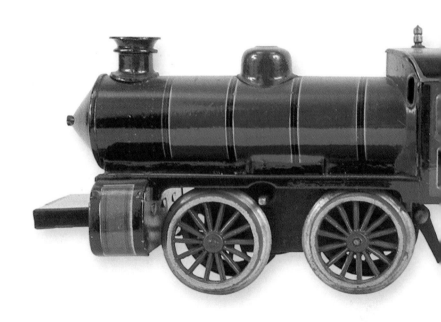

A toy train like this one is really the most basic model. It is a generic 0-4-0 locomotive with tender, 1.9 inch (48 mm) gauge, made by Bing. All model train manufacturers produced inexpensive versions like this, bringing toy trains within the reach of every budget.

As seen on the previous page, model train manufacturers
would produce inexpensive items that children could save
their pennies to buy. The model shown here was
produced just after the First World War by the
French company JEP (Jouet de Paris). It is a small
clockwork train—the key is visible—which must
have reached quite a speed on its
1.4 inch (35 mm) gauge rails.
Note that in comparison
    with the 2-2-0
    locomotive and
    tender, the
    buffers are in
    fact quite
    accurately
    detailed.

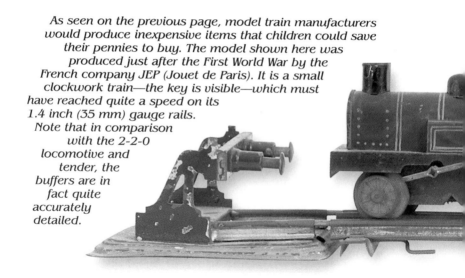

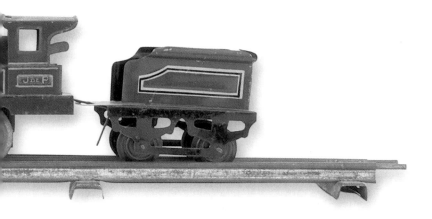

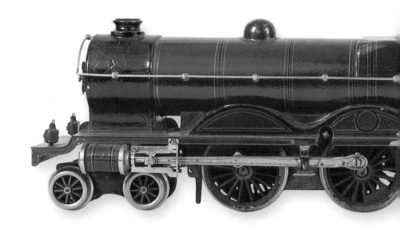

A 4-4-2 NBR Atlantic with a six-wheeled tender, produced by Märklin in about 1910. This was one of the German company's more sophisticated models, made of sheet steel and entirely painted by hand. The letters NBR indicate that this is a model of a North British Railway engine, and the reference 1021 on the cab-side is, in this case, the real engine number in the train company's rolling stock inventory.

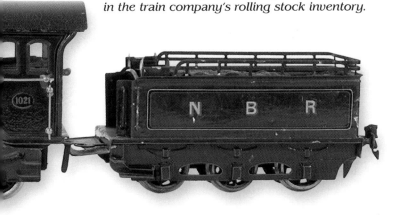

*Another top-of-the-range Märklin mode
dating from 1913. This is a Pacific 4-6-2 wit
a bogie tender, called* The Great Bear. Th
locomotive is powered by steam and

...anks to a fire tube running through the length of the ...oiler, steam puffed out of the funnel just like a real ...comotive. The tender tells us that this train belongs ... Great Western, a well-known British company.

This Pacific 4-6-2 bearing the PLM colors was produced by Märklin in three different versions: one clockwork, one electric, and one steam-powered, like the one pictured here. Note that from 1909, the Pacific 4-6-2 models were produced in their hundreds.

This remarkable bogie tender, perfectly suited to the Pacific 4-6-2, is a marvel of grace and sophistication. Invented in 1832 by John B. Jarvis, bogies are pivoting trucks with springs which allow vehicles to negotiate curves more easily.

This locomotive was made by Hornby
in Liverpool for the French market, as
indicated by the PLM colors. It is a generic
1.4 inch (35 mm) gauge, 0-4-0 locomotive,
typical of the 1920s.

*This 0-4-0 T model is the same as the one
on the preceding page, only the paint
has changed. It was produced in many
different company colors—this model is in the
livery of Britain's London and North Eastern Railway.*

*A fine 1.4 inch (35 mm)
gauge 4-6-2 locomotive
with a six-wheeled tender,
inspired by the Pacific
locomotives of the German
DRG (Deutsche Reichs
bahn Gesellschaft), of
which more than five
hundred were built,
beginning in 1925.
This model runs on
twenty volts. It was sold
by Märklin from the late
1920s and into the 1930s.*

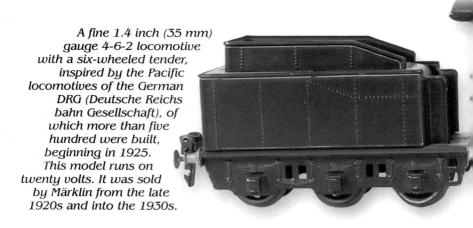

Dating from the late 1920s, this remarkable O scale
electric Pacific 4-6-2 with bogie tender was based on
the German Pacific 01/03 locomotives. The inscription on
the engineer's cab is the manufacturer Märklin's reference
number. Real locomotives were operated by an engineer
and a stoker, and pulled express and semi-fast
passenger trains on the German network.

*This reproduction of the French Pacific
is considered "reasonably accurate" by specialis
electric train collectors. Of the original Wurtemberg
Pacific class C 4-6-2 with bogie tender
forty-one were produced, beginning in 1909*

...is electric model was made by Bing in the 1920s.
...tender of this size was designed to carry 9.9 short
...ns (9 metric tonnes) of coal and 1059 cubic feet
...0 m³) of water, which meant the train could travel for
...> to 190 miles (300 km) without stopping to refuel.

This Märklin 1.9 inch (48 mm) gauge locomotive was based on the Wurtemberg Pacific 4-6-2, but the placement of the wheels is in fact 4-4-0, thus less expensive to reproduce. The bogie tender has been kept.

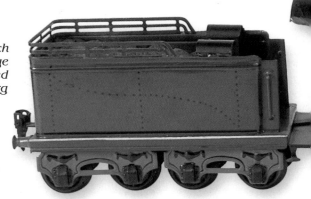

The name of the British Ten Wheels, like this 4-6-0 locomotive, does not include the wheels on the tender—otherwise this would be a Sixteen Wheels, as the tender has three axles! This 1.9 inch (48 mm) gauge model, dating from about 1920, bears the proud name of *Experiment*, which was also the name of the *Brother Jonathan*, the first bogie locomotive. The numbers 66 on the cab and G1020 on the right flank are the manufacturer Märklin's references.

Here is a 4-6-2 locomotive with tender inspired by the 3-1200 (first and second series) of the French company Compagnie du Nord. The large tender is accurately depicted: the original had a capacity of 1307 cubic feet (37 m³). On this locomotive, the door on the smokebox opens. This 0 scale model, measuring 15.8 inches (40 cm), was manufactured between 1928 and 1940 by the French company LR. The original on which this model is based was designed in 1923, and forty-five were built.

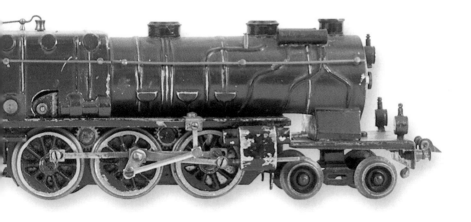

A lovely 1.9 inch (48 mm) gauge reproduction by Bing of a classic British 4-4-0 locomotive of the sort that traveled between London and other cities in the years after 1910, and which must have taken thousands of soldiers home on leave during the First World War. As was common in Britain, the locomotive was given a name— Duke of York.

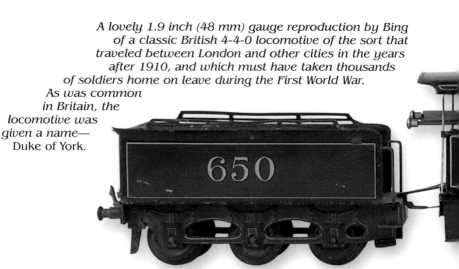

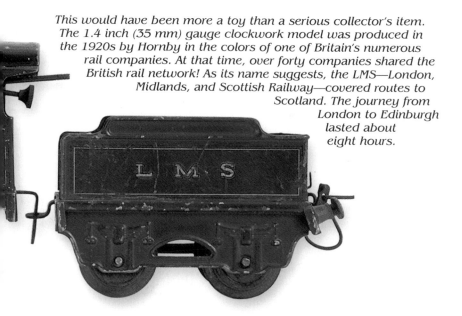

This would have been more a toy than a serious collector's item. The 1.4 inch (35 mm) gauge clockwork model was produced in the 1920s by Hornby in the colors of one of Britain's numerous rail companies. At that time, over forty companies shared the British rail network! As its name suggests, the LMS—London, Midlands, and Scottish Railway—covered routes to Scotland. The journey from London to Edinburgh lasted about eight hours.

The company best known as JEP began operating under the name SIF, which is the name on this bogie tender. SIF produced this mechanical 0-4-0 locomotive during the 1920s in one of its five French factories. The company also had depots throughout the world.

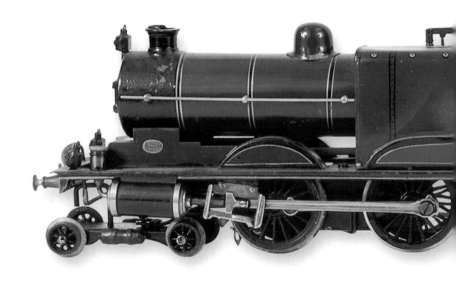

A superb English 4-4-0 II scale, steam-powered locomotive with six-wheeled tender. All the details are accurate, from the gold edging, which adds a touch of real elegance, to the "Midland Wyvern" coat of arms on the cab. Just visible on the front of the engine is the bronze oval plaque that gives the train's origin. The reference 999 on the tender was the train's number in the rolling-stock inventory. The II scale, generally in use before the First World War, is the equivalent of a gauge of 2.1 inches (54 mm).

Similar to the model double on the preceding page, this I scale, 1.8 inch (45 mm) gauge, electric 4-4-0 locomotive, made by Märklin, is typical of the great trains to be seen in Britain between the two World Wars. The founder of this prestigious company, Theodor Friedrich Wilhelm Märklin, was born on April 2, 1817, in the German village of Tieringen.

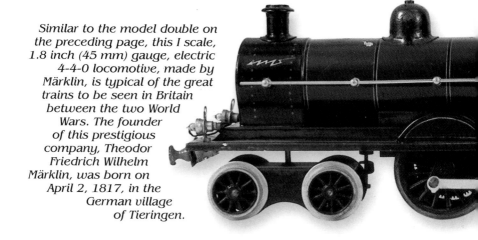

A fine example of a Märklin 0 scale standard German Pacific, with Witte type smoke deflectors and still with its original tender, dating from about 1930. "Standard" in this context means that the trains were built to designs by the German rail company, the Deutsche Reichsbahn Gesellschaft, which united all the former regional companies with the aim of standardizing the German rail network's equipment and rolling stock.

Smoke deflectors are the vertical pieces of tinplate placed at the front and on either side of the locomotive. As their name suggests, they are there to deflect the steam billowing from the funnel upwards, so that it does not obscure the engineer's vision. This clockwork 0 scale 4-4-2 locomotive is based on a German standard 4-6-2, equipped with a bogie tender. It was issued by Märklin in the 1930s.

This 0 scale locomotive is adapted from a German standard steam engine of the 1920s and 1930s. The manufacturer, Fleischmann, shortened the engine considerably, producing a 0-4-0 design with only the two central sets of wheels, as opposed to the 4-6-2, 2-8-2, or 2-10-0 that the original would have had. The firm Fleischmann, founded in the southern German town of Nuremberg in 1906, is still in business today.

In 1940, the Alsace-based company SACM
built five 4-6-4 R and S locomotives. This model,
issued by LR in the 1950s, is an extremely simplified
version of these locomotives—only six of the original
fourteen wheels remain! LR was named after its founder,
Louis Roussy, and its factories, in Paris, produced toy
trains from 1927 to 1957.

This type of Pacific is known as a Wurtemberg, because they were designed and built for the rail network in the German region of the same name, where they were used for pulling express passenger trains. This 1.4 inch (35 mm) gauge model with an electric motor is by Bing; it was made in about 1910.

*The French company JEP took its
inspiration for this model from the
Pacific 3-1280, which, in 1938,
brought the King of England's
royal train to Paris, with King
George V, Queen Elizabeth,
and their two daughters,
Elizabeth, the future queen,
and Margaret, on board.
This Pacific with the
rounded front was extremely
popular; the 1.4 inch (35 mm)
gauge model was on sale from the
late 1930s to the early 1950s.*

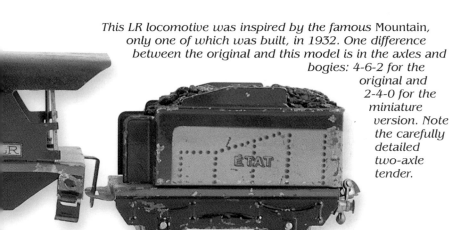

This LR locomotive was inspired by the famous Mountain, *only one of which was built, in 1932. One difference between the original and this model is in the axles and bogies: 4-6-2 for the original and 2-4-0 for the miniature version. Note the carefully detailed two-axle tender.*

Pacifics were first built by the American Locomotive Company, ALCO, for use on the MPRR (Missouri Pacific Railroad) line, which is how they got their name. The first 4-6-2 left the factory in 1895; the name Pacific was adopted in 1902. Apart from the solitary GWR engine, The Great Bear *(see page 78), PLM built the first Pacifics in Europe in 1907. Several series were produced. This JEP 0 scale electric model has the correct distribution of axles (4-6-2) and corresponds to the series of forty-five locomotives built in 1923.*

*Another Pacific 4-6-2, simplified to a
4-4-0 for reasons of expense,
produced by JEP in the 1930s.
It proudly bears the name
of the Compagnie du Nord,
founded in 1845 for train
lines from Paris to towns
in the north of France.*

The JEP catalogs for 1937 to 1940 offered this model for sale, reference 5765 LT. It is a 1.4 inch (35 mm) gauge 4-4-4 model with a rounded front, complete with working headlamp, reverse gear, and a similarly rounded tender. It ran on a 20 volt supply.

Halfway between a model and a toy, this is a splendid reproduction of the Great Western's 4-6-0 King George V, number 6000. It was issued by Märklin in the 1930s. Thirty of the original locomotives were built, starting in 1927. The number 6000 on the door of the engineer's cab was the engine number in the company's rolling stock inventory. The 1.9 inch (48 mm) gauge model has an electric motor and triple-axle tender.

Based on the Pacific 4-6-2, but in a 4-4-2 version, this superb locomotive and bogie tender is an O scale Märklin with only two driving axles. After the death of Märklin's founder, Theodor Märklin, the company was run for many years by his heirs, Eugen and Fritz.

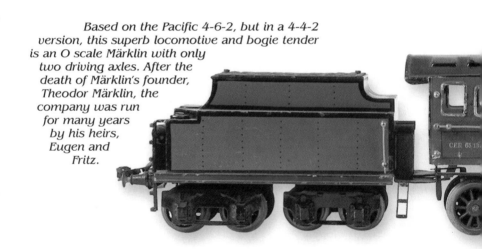

One occasionally comes across locomotives coupled with a tender of a different model. That is the case for this example—a Compagnie du Nord locomotive with an SNCF tender.

Both are French companies, but the first was private, the second state-owned. The Compagnie du Nord was in business from 1845 to 1937, whereas the SNCF was founded in 1938 and is still France's national train operator. Locomotive and tender, both 0 gauge, are by Hornby, the former dating from the 1920s and the latter from the 1950s. The engine is powered by clockwork, the hole for the key is visible between the 0 and R of Nord.

*A superbly detailed reproduction of the
famous Mountain 4-8-2. The single
original was produced by the French
company Fives-Lille in 1931. This
treasure was produced by Märklin
who manufactured a range of trains*

*from basic toys for infants to highly
sophisticated models such as the one
pictured. The engine and tender together
measure 23.2 inches (59 cm) in length.
In the Märklin catalog for 1934, it was
reference ME 66/12920.*

*The British firm Bassett-Lowke, based in Northampton,
made train sets for children between 1889 and 1965.
It produced this electric 4-4-0 in the colors of the
London and North-Eastern Railway during the 1920s.
Bassett-Lowke have recently begun production again and
are currently selling several new models.*

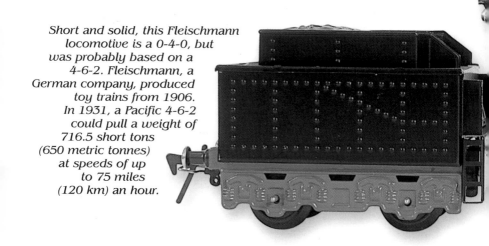

Short and solid, this Fleischmann locomotive is a 0-4-0, but was probably based on a 4-6-2. Fleischmann, a German company, produced toy trains from 1906. In 1931, a Pacific 4-6-2 could pull a weight of 716.5 short tons (650 metric tonnes) at speeds of up to 75 miles (120 km) an hour.

This electric 1.8 inch (45 mm) gauge model takes its inspiration from at least two sources— a PLM Coupe-Vent and a Wurtemberg Pacific, although it is a 4-4-2. It also has a German-style bogie tender.

Today, electric model trains are powered using a transformer which lowers the voltage to a level that presents no danger to children. However, the earliest electric trains were plugged directly into the wall outlet at 110 volts!

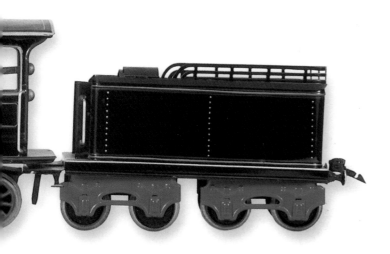

The original of this bogie tender pulled by a smart Fleischmann locomotive had a capacity of 777 cubic feet (22 m³) of water. The locomotive is a reproduction of a German 2-6-2, series 23, which was built in 1944. Note that the central wheel does not have a flange to help the model engine negotiate tight toy-track curves.

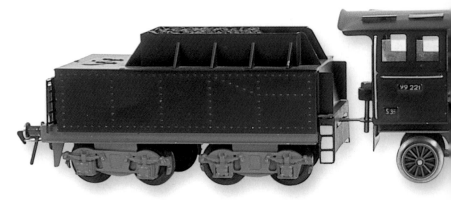

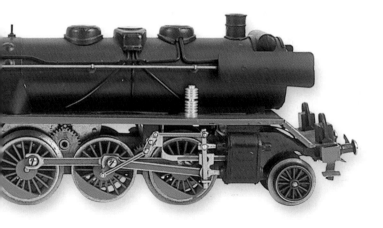

*This extraordinary engine was JEP's swan song. The
company closed in 1968. This model, reference
number 6075, shows an SNCF 2-8-2 P steam locomotive
and bogie tender, both in die-cast metal. They were
produced between 1957 and 1964 in 0 gauge*

he engine and tender together measure roughly 19 inches
8 cm) in length and weigh 6 pounds (2.7 kg). It is a
magnificent example, powered by two AP5 motors driving
ie four driving axles. Beginning in 1942, a total of
18 of the SNCF 2-8-2 P locomotives were built.

*The smoke deflectors of th
locomotive with the rounded fror
typical of the 1930s and 1940
were probably inspired by th
4-6-4 U1 dating from 1949*

*those days, the designers at JEP
oduced a variety of free interpretations
f contemporary trains—authenticity was
ot their prime concern. Nonetheless, their
eations have a charm all their own.*

Like the locomotive on the preceding double page, this 1.4 inch (35 mm) gauge 4-4-2 was based on the rounded forms of 1940s 4-6-4 engines, while the bogie tender is reminiscent of a standard German model. This example was produced by the French firm LR.

*The firm Munier, specializing in mode
rather than toys, sold treasures like th
locomotive in the 1950s. This electr
0 scale, 1.4 inch (35 mm) gauge engin*

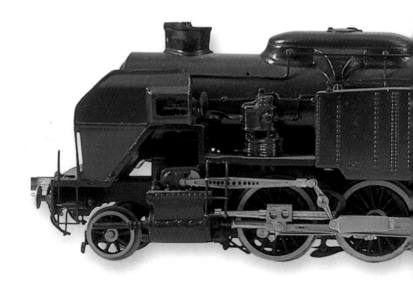

brass and bronze is a 2-8-2 TC
(-1200 Nord). Seventy-two of the
riginal locomotives were built,
eginning in 1932.

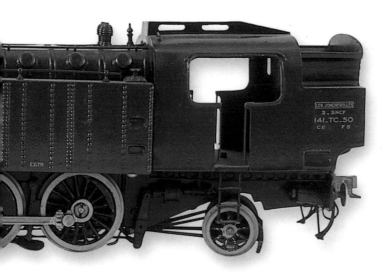

This is another Munier model of rar
quality, made of bronze and brass
painted black. It is a very accurat
copy of a 4-6-2 C (3-1200 Nord) wit
a bogie tender. Forty of the origina
locomotives were built, beginning in 192

Munier only produced models of French locomotives and other French vehicles, always in very small quantities, and to astonishingly high standards of accuracy compared with ordinary toy trains.

Here we have a 0 gauge locomotive
made by Hornby. It is a British 0-4-0 T
model adapted for the French market, with
the initials of the French national train company,
SNCF, founded in 1938, on the flank of the engine.

*This very basic 1.4 inch (35 mm) gauge
model takes its inspiration from the
steam locomotives of the 1930s. It was
marketed from 1934 to 1937 by JEP.
It measures nearly 10 inches (25 cm) in length
and was also available in dark brown, used
by France's Compagnie du Nord for its express
trains. This model has remote-controlled
automatic forward and reverse gears.*

This 1.4 inch (35 mm) gauge Rapide LR is not a copy of any particular train, but it is exceedingly fine nonetheless! With its warm blue color, and despite the very basic wheel system (0-4-0), it was a very popular present for little boys in the late 1930s. Although not nearly as splendid as a top-of-the-range Märklin, it did have the advantage of being far cheaper.

This little locomotive was manufactured by LR in the 1950s, when one might have seen little boys trundling a similar engine around the local park. It is based on a 5.51 short tons (5 metric tonnes) narrow gauge (23.6 inch or 60 cm) Decauville, although this model has an almost cartoon-like feel to it.

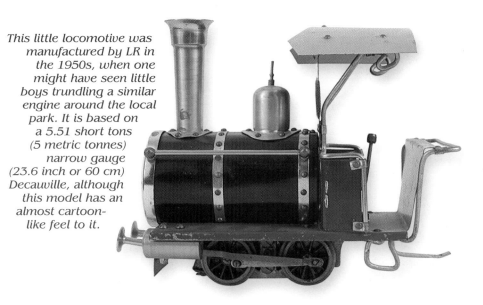

Note the hole in the flank of this locomotive's boiler for the key to wind up the clockwork mechanism. Fully wound up, this LR 1.4 inch (35 mm) gauge locomotive would whiz three times around the track before grinding to a halt. It is based on a standard SNCF engine of the 1950s.

One of a number of versions of JEP's 0-4-0/2-4-0 locomotive with a rounded nose, produced in large numbers between 1938 and 1950. Its catalog reference was 4321 LT. The locomotive and tender together measure nearly 10 inches (25 cm), with the engine accounting for 6 of them (15 cm). Note that in this photograph, the four-wheeled tender was coupled to the locomotive back-to-front!

This impressive Aster I scale brass engine was designed for a 2.6 inch (67 mm) gauge track. It is based on an American four-coupled Shay—an articulated forest locomotive— dating from the 1920s. Supported on bogies and driven by a lay-shaft, this engine could cope with the rough, often temporary track laid on "logging lines."

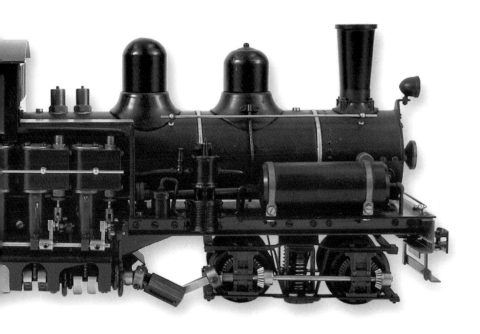

*This is a rather comical 0-4-0 version of an
electric locomotive belonging to the Central
London Railway. Made of painted tinplate,
it measures 6 inches (15 cm) long and dates from
the beginning of the twentieth century, the original
having been built in 1903. The manufacturer is
Bing, and it is a I scale model.*

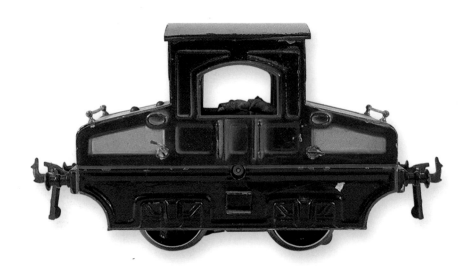

This is a model of an early London Underground District Line electric Märklin locomotive.
It is called a BB because of the placement of its axles—it has two bogies with two axles each.
This model dates from the first decade of the twentieth century.

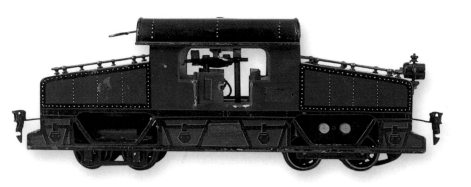

*This electric locomotive was known as
a "salt box" because its shape is reminiscent
of the salt and pepper boxes from our grandparents'
kitchen cupboards. The model shown is a 1.9 inch
(48 mm) gauge locomotive by Bing.*

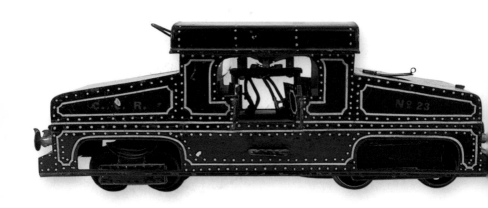

This style of locomotive was also used in France, as shown by this Bing model dating from shortly after 1910. It is in the colors of the Paris-Orleans (PO) line, and the reference E1 on the door of the cab corresponds to its place in the series E1 to E8.

Eight of these BB locomotives were built (numbered one to eight) for the Paris-Orleans line. This superb Märklin scale I reproduction is perfect in every detail: even the "rivets" are all hand-painted to make them stand out.

This model, along with many others in this book, can be seen at the Rambolitrain museum in Rambouillet, south-west of Paris (see page 374).

Toys, like everything in life, follow the fashions and technological trends of the day. This CR O scale electric locomotive first appeared in shop windows as a result of the success of the BB locomotive in the 1920s.

During the 1920s, electric locomotives conquered the rails, and inspired many toy makers, including Bing. The German firm produced this four-wheeled 1.4 inch (35 mm) gauge wind-up locomotive between 1920 and 1930.

The earliest experiments with electric traction date back to the beginning of the nineteenth century in the United States and France. This Märklin model with two pantographs is based on the first trains used in various regions of Germany in the early days of rail travel.

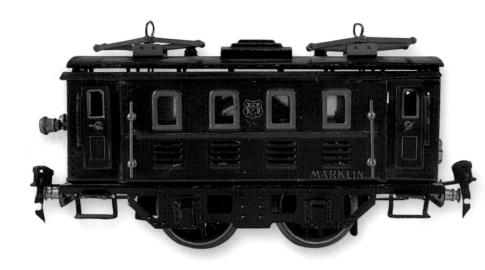

Unlike the model shown on the facing page,
this late 1920s locomotive, also by Märklin,
has a single pantograph. It is a simplified
B-type I gauge version of the Swiss engines
operating on the Saint Gotthard line.

*Some children adored the great express steam trains
taking hordes of vacationers to the Riviera, while
others preferred the quiet romance of the suburban train.
It was for the latter that this 1.4 inch (35 mm) gauge
BB fourgon was produced by CR in the 1920s.
Its two pantographs and central operating
lever can be clearly seen in the photograph.*

This is a simplified Hornby model of a BB locomotive belonging to the London Metropolitan Railway. The term BB indicates two bogies, each with two axles. This system of classification applies to both electric and diesel locomotives. For steam engines, the number and placement of the axles are indicated by a series of numbers (for example, 4-6-2 or 2-8-2).

It is hard to imagine the number of hours of intensive labor that must have gone into such a detailed model as this. Small wonder that the price of such a treasure was sometimes on the high side. This Märklin electric 2C1 represents the Swiss Ae 6/12-2, of which 114 were built in total, beginning in 1921. These machines were only taken out of active use at the end of the 1980s.

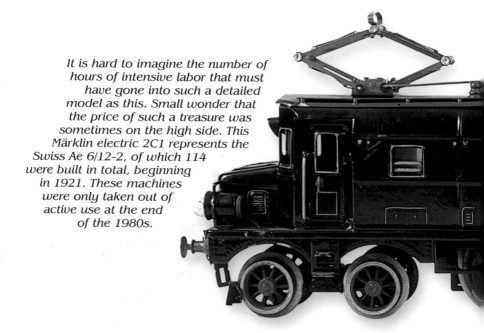

The Fliegender Hamburger *is not a new item on a fast-food menu, but the name of this diesel automatic, only ever produced as a single prototype in 1932.*

It was the first experiment using a diesel motor on a railcar of this sort. Other, improved versions followed. This model has an electric, not diesel, engine.

*A magnificent Hornby reproduction of one of
the finest post-war railcars, by Bugatti, on three
sets of two axles. Two of these railcars were
built in 1936. The idea came from the great
businessman Ettore Bugatti, as a way of
recouping the funds invested in the Bugatti
Royale, and to provide work for his factories in
the dark days of the 1930s depression.*

The initiative was supported by Raoul Dautry, who was at that time head of the French state rail company, hence the word état, meaning "state," painted at each end of the railcar. In 1934, one of the Bugatti railcars broke the world speed record for a train, attaining a speed of 120 miles (192 km) per hour.

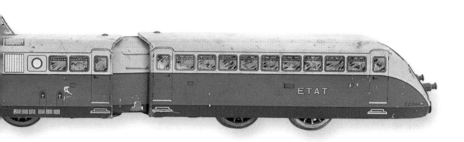

This American diesel articulated locomotive goe
by the name of City of Portland. *It operated o*
the route between New York and Washington

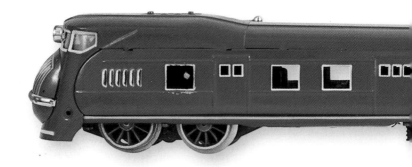

*his model was issued by Paya, a Spanish
rm specializing in tinplate toys, sometime
the late 1930s.

Michelin makes tires, as everyone knows. This charming model of the Micheline n. 5, appropriately enough, has strips of rubber around the wheels, though it was indeed designed to drive on rails. This O scale model was made by LR in the 1930s, and measures 15.8 inches (40 cm). In 1931, the Micheline demonstrated its capacities on a stretch of track between Paris and the fashionable seaside resort of Deauville, in Normandy, reaching an average speed of nearly 67 miles (109 km) per hour.

The 1930s were exceptionally fertile in terms of design; this electric railcar with a propeller, made by Kruckenberg, is a fine example. Only one full-size locomotive was ever built, in 1930, reproduced a year or two later by Märklin as an 0 or I gauge model. This "zeppelin on rails," as it was known because of its shape, originally had two twin-axle bogies, although this model only has two single axles. The same firm re-issued this marvelous engine in 1999, as an H0 scale model.

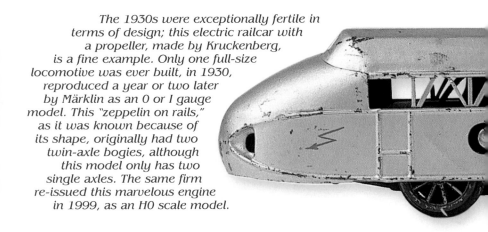

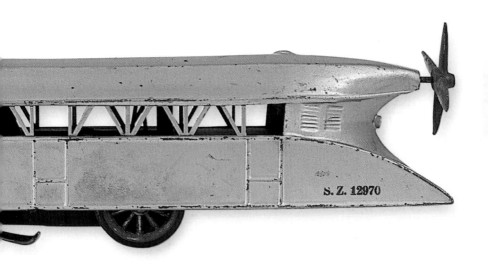

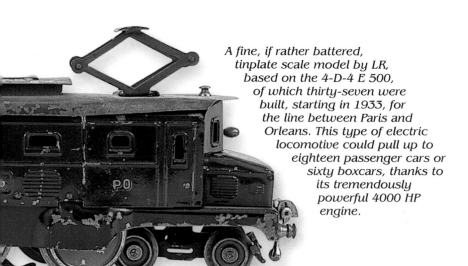

A fine, if rather battered, tinplate scale model by LR, based on the 4-D-4 E 500, of which thirty-seven were built, starting in 1933, for the line between Paris and Orleans. This type of electric locomotive could pull up to eighteen passenger cars or sixty boxcars, thanks to its tremendously powerful 4000 HP engine.

*A charmingly childish, chubby,
short version of a 2-D-2 500
operating on the Paris-Orleans
network in France. This Hornby model
dates from the second half of the 1930s.*

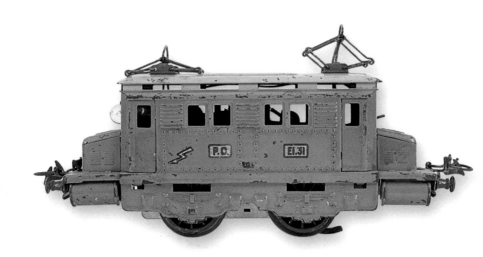

*The walkways on this electric locomotive
made by LR can be folded up or down.
Shown here is a 0 gauge (1.4 inch, or 35 mm)
BB 1-80. Eighty of these locomotives were built,
beginning in 1924, for the Paris-Orleans rail network.*

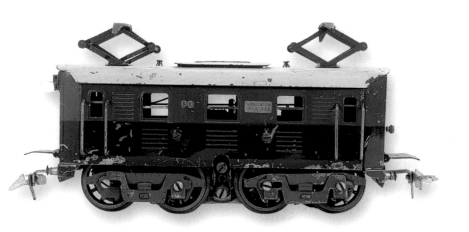

The model train specialist Guy Landgraf
explains that this 1930s 0 gauge
model electric locomotive, made by LR
and based on an engine built in 1900,
was specially designed to climb slopes.

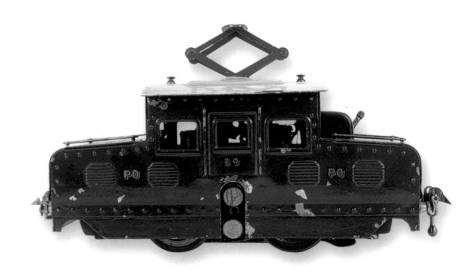

*Here is a 2-B-2 adaptation of a German
E18 1-D-1 locomotive. It has only four
driving wheels, as opposed to eight for the
full-size engine. Made by Märklin, it is an 0 gauge
model and dates from the late 1940s or early 1950s.*

In its early days, when the company's founder Louis Renault was still in charge, Renault made not only cars, but also trucks, tractors, boats, airplanes, and trains. The firm produced 239 railcars of the type shown here between 1935 and 1948. It was a golden era for the company, when its airplanes won races and its trains broke speed records. In 1935, the Renault shown here maintained an average speed of some 86 miles (138 km) per hour, with a top speed of over 100 miles (160 km) per hour, on the journey from Paris to Mulhouse and back. These two models of the Renault ABJ1 railcar were issued by LR in the 1940s.

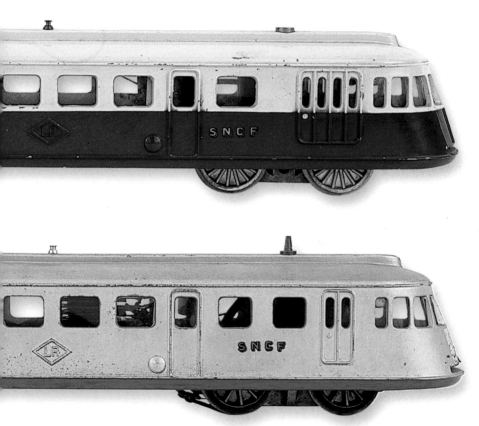

*An articulated electric railcar by Fleischmann,
modeled on the German ET 25 railcars built after 1935,
which were used mainly in the suburbs of large cities.*

Each country has their own distinctive model trains
and Spain is no exception. The Spanish firm Paya
was founded in Ibi, near Alicante, by Raimund Paya

*Among its products was this 1950s 0 scale,
painted tinplate model, based on a
mid-1930s American diesel.*

*American trains are certainly glamorous, with their
streamlined aerodynamic form and their single
headlight boldly shining above the engineer's
windshield. The model shown below is a*

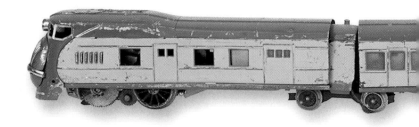

*eproduction of one of the pre-war American diesels,
nade in the 1950s by the Spanish manufacturer Paya.
Trains like this were used on long-distance journeys
departing from Boston or Los Angeles.*

This is a model of a German diesel-electric railcar with two 400 hp engines at 1400 rpm. This type of engine would use up 6.3 ounces (180 grams) o

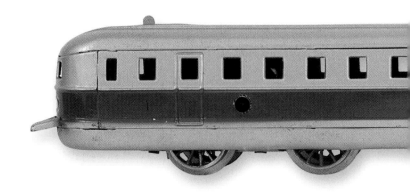

uel per hp unit per hour—an enormous amount,
*especially bearing in mind that one train could
be made up of several of these cars.*

The TAR (the French initials for train automoteur rapide *or Rapid Electric Railcar) was a railcar with three cars that was first put into operation in 1934 on routes across France and into Switzerland. They were withdrawn from active use in the late 1950s. This is a 0 gauge JEP model with only one car. The model was manufactured between 1954 and 1966 as reference JEP 6085. The signal box in lithographed tinplate is also by JEP, reference 5358.*

POSTE N°4

With its body in zamac, this locomotive is an exact copy of the original BB 8100 (this is number BB-8101, as indicated by the painted plaque on the side) used by the SNCF. Starting in 1949, 171 of the full-size locomotives were built, some of which are still in use. It is estimated that each of these locomotives has traveled over 3,750,000 miles (6,000,000 km). The model shown is by JEP, reference 6067, with a single motor and eight driving wheels, manufactured between 1953 and 1964.

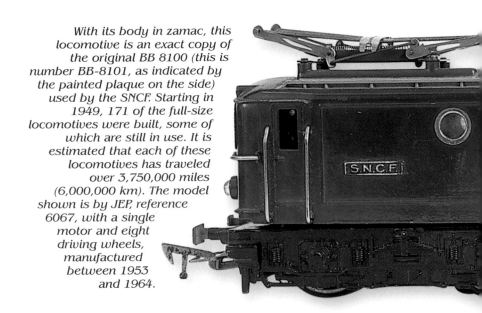

Like the model shown on the preceding double page, this copy of the SNCF's CC 7001 locomotive is by JEP. It is also made of zamac—an alloy of zinc, aluminum, magnesium, antimony, and copper, hence the name. This 0 gauge model, catalog reference JEP 6077, was produced between 1952 and 1964. It has two AP 5 motors and twelve driving wheels! Catalog reference JEP 6076 is simpler, and only has one motor.

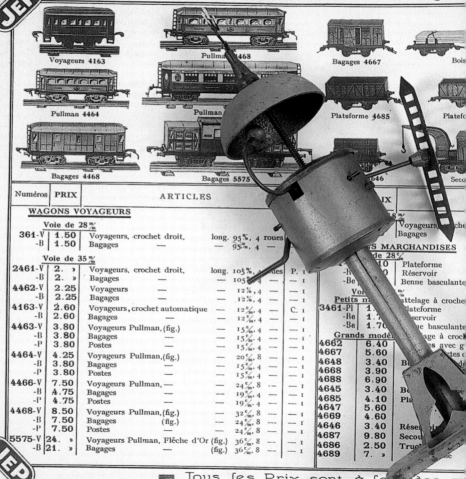

Voyageurs 4163

Pullman 4468

Bagages 4667

Bois

Pullman 4464

Pullman

Plateforme 4685

Platefo

Bagages 4468

Bagages 5575

646

Seco

Numéros	PRIX	ARTICLES				IX
WAGONS VOYAGEURS						Voyageurs, che
Voie de 28 m/m						Bagages
361-V	1.50	Voyageurs, crochet droit,	long. 95 %, 4 roues			**S MARCHANDISES**
-B	1.50	Bagages —	— 95 m, 4 —			de 28 m/m
Voie de 35 m/m						Plateforme
2461-V	2. »	Voyageurs, crochet droit,	long. 105½%, 4 roues	P. I		Réservoir
-B	2. »	Bagages —	— 105 m, 4 —	— I		Benne basculante
4462-V	2.25	Voyageurs —	— 12 %, 4 —	— I		Vo m/m
-B	2.25	Bagages —	— 12 %, 4 —	— I		Petits m uttelage à croche
4163-V	2.60	Voyageurs, crochet automatique	— 12 m, 4 —	C. I	3461-Pl	Plateforme
-B	2.60	Bagages —	— 12 m, 4 —		-Re	Réservoir
4463-V	3.80	Voyageurs Pullman, (fig.)	— 15 c/m, 4 —	— I	-Be 1.70	e basculante
-B	3.80	Bagages —	— 15 m, 4 —	— I	Grands modè	age à croc
-P	3.80	Postes —	— 15 m, 4 —	— I	4662 6.40	es avec g
4464-V	4.25	Voyageurs Pullman, (fig.)	— 20 c/m, 8 —	— I	4667 5.60	rtes
-B	3.80	Bagages —	— 15 m, 4 —	— I	4648 3.40	B
-P	3.80	Postes —	— 15 m, 4 —	— I	4668 3.90	
4466-V	7.50	Voyageurs Pullman, —	— 24 c/m, 8 —	— I	4688 6.90	
-B	4.75	Bagages —	— 19 %, 4 —	— I	4645 3.40	B
-P	4.75	Postes —	— 19 %, 4 —	— I	4685 4.10	Pl
4468-V	8.50	Voyageurs Pullman, (fig.)	— 32 c/m, 8 —	— I	4647 5.60	
-B	7.50	Bagages (fig.)	— 24 m, 8 —	— I	4669 4.60	
-P	7.50	Postes —	— 24 m, 8 —	— I	4646 3.40	Réser
5575-V	24. »	Voyageurs Pullman, Flêche d'Or (fig.)	— 36 c/m, 8 —	— I	4687 9.80	Secou
-B	21. »	Bagages —	(fig.) 36 c/m, 8 —	— I	4686 2.50	Truc
						4689 7. »

II

model trains
LARGE-SCALE
CARS

A few years ago, it seemed as if train travel had had its day. More and more people could afford their own car, which seemed so much more convenient; and affordable air travel to distant destinations cut hours, if not days, off the journey. Yet the train has rallied, and its environmental benefits, speed, and convenience are making it attractive once again. From the ordinary suburban train to the most luxurious Pullman on the Orient Express, the range of styles is remarkable. You will find some splendid examples—mainly 0 and I scale—in the following pages.

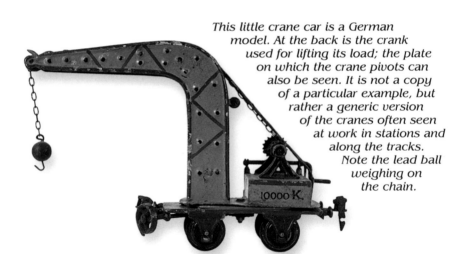

This little crane car is a German model. At the back is the crank used for lifting its load; the plate on which the crane pivots can also be seen. It is not a copy of a particular example, but rather a generic version of the cranes often seen at work in stations and along the tracks. Note the lead ball weighing on the chain.

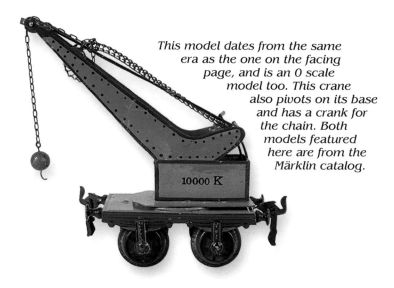

This model dates from the same era as the one on the facing page, and is an 0 scale model too. This crane also pivots on its base and has a crank for the chain. Both models featured here are from the Märklin catalog.

10000 K

*This copy of the earliest cars with bogies from
the Paris Métro was made in around 1905, and
is a faithful imitation of the original, which
transformed the lives of ordinary Parisians
in the early years of the twentieth century.
Made by FV, it is an 0 scale model.*

A first-class bogie passenger car dating from some time after 1910. Although the I scale model is of a British car, it was made in Germany, by Märklin.

Two 0 scale high-sided cars manufactured by the German firm Bing in the late nineteenth century. On the facing page, note the small brakeman's cab, providing shelter from inclement weather. On this page, the car is equipped with stanchions—pieces of wood or metal designed to hold tall loads, like logs or boxes, in place.

With its two walkways at either end,
this Märklin 0 scale car on axles dates
from the first decade of the twentieth century.

*This model of a boxcar is some
ten years older, dating from the 1890s.
It was made by FV, and is a 1.9 inch (48 mm)
gauge model. This gauge was frequently
used by French and German manufacturers
until the mid-1920s.*

These three cars in a row represent, from left to right, an openwork boxcar, a car with a brake, and a side tipper for use on building sites.

The model on the left is by Märklin, and the other two are by Bing. All are O scale models and were probably produced between 1890 and 1908.

These two models are not based on any particular model, but are rather a generic evocation of the type of car in use during the 1880s, when these two cars, both 1.3 inch (33 mm) gauge.

were produced by Märklin. On the left, a boxcar, and right, an openwork car. Children must have loved playing with them, filling them with toy soldiers or zoo animals.

*It is delightful to imagine this little
passenger train on its tinplate rails in
a child's nursery in the late nineteenth
century. It is a rather simplified version*

*f a German passenger train used on
econdary routes, composed of cars with
ide doors and, on the right, a boxcar.
lade by Märklin, it is an 0 scale model.*

On secondary routes, passenger cars were ofte
pretty basic. These two tinplate cars by Märkl
illustrate this point; they represent cars with

wooden body which were used on rack railroads
n the early years of the twentieth century.
These models were sold from about 1920 on.

*With its little trapdoor opening on the side,
this German I scale car was produced by the
German firm Schoenner. It dates from the first
decade of the 1900s, and must have given
hours of pleasure to generations
of children who used it to transport
everything from sand to toy soldiers.*

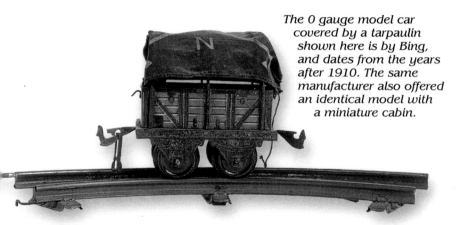

The 0 gauge model car covered by a tarpaulin shown here is by Bing, and dates from the years after 1910. The same manufacturer also offered an identical model with a miniature cabin.

A first-class British passenger car dating from the very beginning of the twentieth century, produced by Märklin as an 0 gauge model some time shortly after 1910.

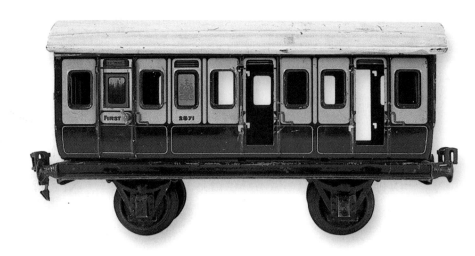

*This model is based on the superb originals
with teak bodies used by the French firm
CIWL—the Compagnie Internationale des
Wagons-Lits—in the late nineteenth and early
twentieth century. This 1.9 inch (48 mm) gauge
Märklin model is the dining car—inside one
can see the tables and chairs.*

*Like the car on the preceding page,
this toy is also based on the teak dining
cars used by the firm CIWL. But while the
first example shown was by Märklin, this one
was produced by its rival company Bing.
The I scale model was on sale in the late
nineteenth and early twentieth century.*

A third version of the teak dining car, this time in lithographed tinplate and produced by Märklin. Note that the roof opens so that the lucky owner can place the miniature passengers inside.

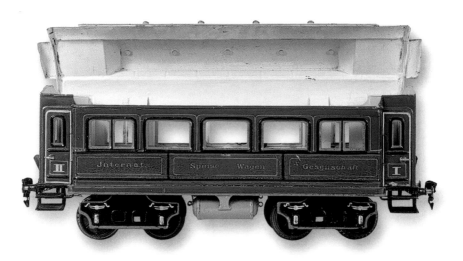

Bearing in mind that O scale trains are all around 1/43 real size, children could couple together toys by different manufacturers on the same track. Here we have a flatcar and tank by the same company, Märklin. Neither is based on a particular original, but are rather general versions of the style of the period.

As with the tank on the facing page, camouflaged like the FT Renault used in the First World War, this cannon is not based on a particular original. This O gauge Märklin model, like the ones featured opposite, dates from the 1920s.

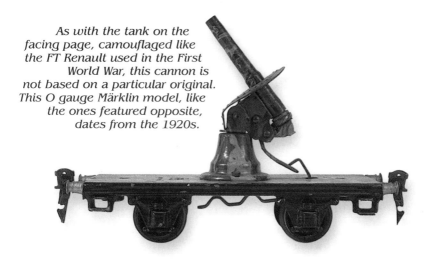

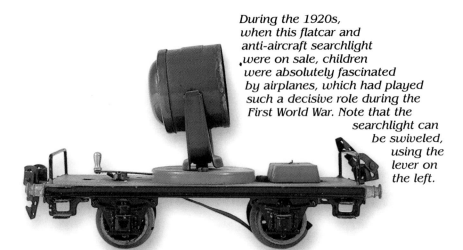

During the 1920s, when this flatcar and anti-aircraft searchlight were on sale, children were absolutely fascinated by airplanes, which had played such a decisive role during the First World War. Note that the searchlight can be swiveled, using the lever on the left.

*The label visible on this car, bearing
the name of Standard House, G. Christiaensen,
Antwerp, is not an original feature of the
model. It must have been placed there by
a shopkeeper. Like the model on the facing
page, this 0 scale wagon used for
transporting cannons is by Märklin.*

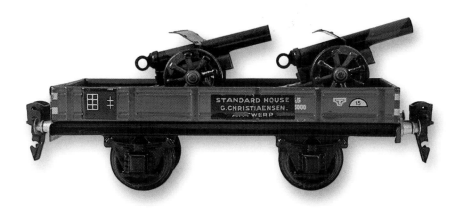

A superb reproduction by Märklin of a car used on the French PLM company's main lines. One hundred and twenty of the originals were built after 1913. It is a bogie baggage car surmounted by a central lookout, and even has working sliding doors. This magnificent large scale model measures about 17.7 inches (45 cm) in length.

This car is a 0 gauge model inspired by the Standard electric railcars (series 3, 4, and 5) used on lines from Paris's Saint Lazare station to the suburbs. More than three hundred of the originals were built after 1924. The model shown was manufactured by CR, the company founded by Charles Rossignol, which produced lithographed tinplate toys from 1868.

An 0 scale hopper car made in England by Bing in the 1920s. These cars, used for transporting supplies of minerals, varied in capacity. As the words painted on this example indicate, the original for this model had a capacity of 22 short tons (20 metric tonnes).

*A German standard car based on a
CIWL dining car. Made by Märklin,
this O scale model was made
in Germany between the wars.*

Mitropa—or Mittel Europa Gesellschaft, to give it its full name—was a rival company of CIWL. This car was produced by Karl Bubb in two versions, 0 and I scale. Other manufacturers, like Märklin, produced similar cars painted in the colors of various companies.

Most model train manufacturers strove to attai
as high a degree of accuracy as possible
However, they had to adapt certain detail
such as the proportional length of the ca

...and, as a result the number of windows. Otherwise the result would have been unpleasing to the eye. The example shown is a 1.9 inch (48 mm) gauge model by Märklin, dating from about 1920.

*At the end of many real trains was
car with a compartment for th
guard and the passengers' luggage
This fine example of a car from*

London's Metropolitan Railway, from around
1910, was manufactured by Hornby and would
make a high-quality companion to the rather
cheap electric engine model on page 171.

Produced by Märklin, this car for first- and second-class passengers is similar to German standard cars from the early 1930s. It is an 0 scale bogie car, and features a wealth of hand-painted detail.

*Whether used for milk, as on the
facing page, or motor oil, as here,
tank cars were an indispensable
part of the rail network. The well-known
company Castrol was founded in 1899 by
C.C. Wakefield; it sold Castrol motor oil,
a castor oil product, from 1909.*

The Castrol tank car on the facing page was by Hornby; the 0 gauge car below is by Bing. Both are in lithographed tinplate, and were sold from 1935 on. At the base of the tank can be seen the letters GW, which stand for the British company Great Western.

An 0 scale Shell tank car on two separate axles
made by Hornby and on sale in the 1920s.
Before entering the oil business, Shell actually
began as a company dealing in shells,
much used in nineteenth-century
jewelry and marquetry.

*Another 0 scale tank car by Hornby,
which appeared in the company's 1930 catalog.
This one transported oil for British Petroleum, one of
the first companies to transport crude oil from Iran.*

To transport logs, a side-loading flatcar is perfect.
This model—complete with sticks that, to scale,
become mighty logs—was sold by Fleischmann
in the late 1930s.

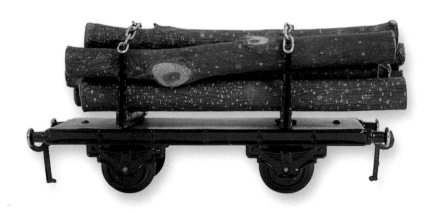

*Like the model featured on the facing page,
this 0 scale car with a real canvas
tarpaulin was manufactured by Fleischmann.
It would have been on sale in about 1938.*

*In the old days, impecunious passengers could travel
in third class, which was in fact not very different from
second class. Here we see a 0 gauge version by
Fleischmann of the German standard cars of the 1920s.
The originals for this model were manufactured
in their hundreds, and were a common sight
on the German rail network.*

This is a German kühlwagen, or refrigerated car. Made as an 0 scale model by Fleischmann, this charming model has a cab on the right and sliding doors to load the goods into the van.

From the early 1930s on, engineers became more and more focused on the question of aerodynamics. This progress is clearly reflected in this JEP 0 scale bogie baggage car, not based on a particular original, but a generic version of cars of the day. Note its rounded, smooth shape.

The letters NE on the side of this car stand for North Eastern, a British railway company. This is a reasonably faithful rendition of a particular British car and a typical tinplate model of the 1930s and 1940s by Hornby.

A voxcar, in the colors of Crawford's Biscuits, supplier of biscuits to the royal family, whose coat of arms can be seen. Another biscuit company, Huntley & Palmer's, also had a lithographed tinplate car in their colors, which is much sought after by collectors. This 1920s 0 scale model is by Hornby.

*This 0 gauge tank car on axles was made
by Fleischmann, based in the German town of
Nuremberg, from 1938 on. Esso took its name from
the initials of Standard Oil, the company that made
the Rockefellers their great fortune.*

Hornby's collection of freight cars is charming and cheery, with its bright colors advertising more or less well-known companies. Colas specialized in "drives and paths," as stated on the logo. This O scale tank car dates from the 1920s.

*We couldn't feature German trains without showing
at least one devoted to transporting great Bavarian beer.
The 0 gauge model shown is by Fleischmann,
and appeared in the company's catalog for 1938.
Note the doors that really open.*

A German car for second and third class passengers. On the unified German rail network, such cars were in common use after 1929. Made by Fleischmann in 1938, this model has doors that open to allow tiny passengers to take a seat inside.

The original for this bogie Pullman was first produced in 1926, and a total of 130 were made. JEP came up with this model in the early 1930s; it is an accurate, if a trifle poetic, 0 scale model of a car that ran between London and various continental cities, using ferries to cross the Channel.

*A Mitropa sleeping car made by Märklin in
the 1930s in two versions—I and 0 gauge.
This bogie car is a rather loose interpretation
of the original.*

*The letters GFN on the right of this 0 scale model
tank car dating from about 1938 may be
the logo of Fleischmann, based in Nuremberg.
In that case, the number beneath the letters
may be a catalog serial number.*

Seen from the side, this tank car looks rather like a truck, with the brakeman's cab at the front of the tank. As the logo indicates, this is a British Petroleum 0 gauge tank car, made by Fleischmann.

This bogie car is based on an original used by the French postal service, three hundred of which were in use after 1928. JEP issued this lovely 0 scale model, which appeared in its catalog during the 1930s and 1940s.

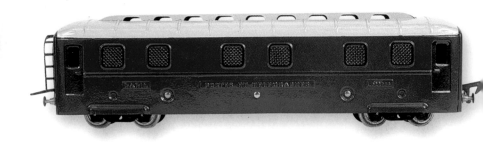

A very elegant German-style bogie car that is reminiscent of a CIWL Pullman car. It was available from Märklin from the early 1930s.

The Swiss railways also had fine originals to copy, such as this second-class bogie car made by Märklin in about 1930. This is in fact a basic model which was also available to the Belgian, French, and Italian markets.

A typical four-wheeled British open freight car in the colors of the Great Northern. 0 gauge, it was produced by Märklin in the 1930s, and was mainly aimed at the British market.

Twenty or so Flèche d'Or cars were built for the Compagnie du Nord from 1928 on. These 35.3 short tons (32 metric tonnes) cars were specially designed for transporting baggage, and the crates could be transferred to ships without being unloaded. JEP issued this realistic 0 scale model in lithographed tinplate.

Dating from the 1950s, this French STEF refrigerator
car is extremely accurate in every detail. It is an
0 scale model by Hornby. Hundreds of these axle
cars were used on all parts of the French rail network.
This model in particular was also produced in an
HO scale version by Hornby, Jouef, and JL.

Another Hornby creation, this four-wheeled car was produced to transport milk to eastern regions of France (as shown by the small label France Est). Although printed with slats (which allowed cool air to circulate through the gaps) it is, in fact, a straightforward boxcar. This 0 scale model dates from the 1940s.

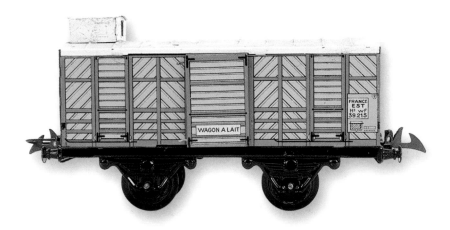

Model trains can be decorated with intricate
logos using lithography on tinplate, as the body
is lithographed before being stamped into shape.
This 0 gauge car was made by Hornby from
the end of the Second World War to the early 1950s.
The original was used for transporting bananas.

An English 0 scale tank car dating from the 1940s, made by Hornby in Liverpool. Pratts was a brand of beer.

*A rather free interpretation (in SNCF colors)
of a narrow-gauge Decauville car for use
on building sites. It is a 0 gauge side tipper,
made by Hornby in the 1950s.*

*Based on the same principle as the Decauville
four-wheeled car on the facing page, this
0 scale side tipper does not correspond to a
particular original. It was made by Hornby
shortly after the Second World War.*

Nearly every oil company had its
own miniature tank car. This one,
proudly displaying the Azur logo,
was manufactured for the French
market by Hornby. Azur took its
name from the practice of the day
of coloring ordinary fuel pink,
and super grade a deep azure
shade, to reduce fraud.
In 1994, Haxo also issued
an 0 scale tank car in Azur's
colors based on a
1920s original.

The Spanish firm Paya has been in the toy business for many years. During the 1950s, it sold the two tank cars featured on these two pages, which would have contained gas or other liquid products. The fortunate owner of this toy could unscrew the stopper on the top of the tank and fill it with liquid, and then empty it through the tube at the base of the tank.

This Paya 0 scale model is similar to the one on the facing page, but differs in that the color has changed and the logo is now hardly visible, and on the right hand side is a brakeman's cab.

As the logo indicates, this 0 scale boxcar
with opening hatches would have
transported cement. It was produced by
Hornby and dates from the 1950s.

This unusually shaped bogie car with the
Arbel logo is a mineral car. Made of
lithographed tinplate, it dates from the 1940s.

While this luxurious Pullman car is, broadly speaking, accurate, the original would have had seven windows, not five as on this 0 scale model. It is nonetheless a splendid reproduction of a CIWL Pullmann car, produced by JEP during the 1950s. Any little boy would be absolutely thrilled to find this under the Christmas tree, along with the locomotive to pull it! The original for this car was manufactured in 1929, and 34 were produced in total.

Because of its rounded shape and the ridges on the roof
this first-class car was known to French train enthusiasts
as a "sausage." Four of these cars were built in 1936
but it was not until the 1950s that JEP manufactured

a far greater quantity of these 0 gauge models! The original had eight windows instead of the model's six. The end windows are similar in shape to those in the CIWL Pullman car featured on the preceding double page.

This car is a distant relation to the CIWL rolling stock, but is actually a generic version of passenger car styles of the period. This model was made by the Spanish firm Paya in the 1970s.

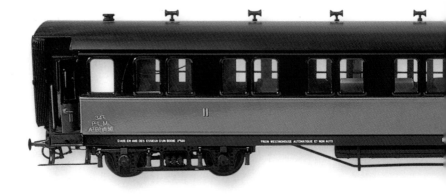

This magnificent PLM car is definitely a model and not a toy. It is an I scale, painted brass model produced by Wilag in the 1980s, representing a PLM first and second class passenger car of the early years of the twentieth century. The number of windows is accurate, giving the model as a whole a long, lean look.

This 0 scale first-class Sprague car could have been seen in days gone by in the Paris Métro. This model was issued by the French firm AS in the 1980s. The original was a familiar sight for Parisians in the 1930s. In fact, these cars had an extremely long working life: some were only withdrawn in the last twenty years. AS also came up with similar models in CMP and Nord-Sud colors.

III

model trains
HO SCALE
LOCOMOTIVES

H0 scale models came to dominate the world of model trains in the 1950s. This new scale was half as big as the older 0 scale (HO stands for half zero). This innovation brought prices tumbling at a stroke, bringing basic train kits within the reach of even the most modest budgets. Another advantage was that the new H0 scale models took up far less room. No longer was model train collecting only for the wealthy and privileged. The introduction of the new scale also ushered in a new age of technological progress and minute attention to detail. In the 1950s, along with the rest of the world, model train collecting entered the modern era.

Our first model in this section is a Fleischmann 2-4-0, a copy of the 35.3 short tons (32 metric tonnes) locomotive and tender 1B h2, of which some 125 were built in total. Note its Heusinger connecting rods and the detail paid to the tubing. This model is also equipped with a remote control reverse function.

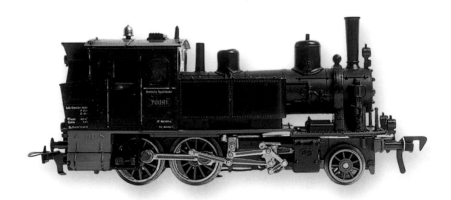

Many versions of 0-6-0 locomotives were produced, both in Europe and America. Often, these engines were given a name—not necessarily an official one, but often all the more affectionate for it. The example shown below was manufactured by Rivarossi.

*This Fleischmann model is a copy of the French
company SACM's 0-10-0 TA. Its usual name was T16
Prusse, and the original was built in 1919. The model
shown was produced by Fleischmann in 1979.*

This famous 4-6-0 No. 590 steam locomotive attained the same record speeds as the Bugatti railcar on the journey from Paris to the port of Le Havre in Normandy. The version shown is a 4-6-0 F, also known as a P8 Prusse, designed by the well-known engineer Garbe. This version was produced by Fleischmann.

Perhaps the most exciting thing about steam
locomotives is that all their workings are on the
outside: tubes, cylinders, funnel, wheels, engineer's
cab—the complete opposite of a modern train like
the TGV or the Japanese Shinkansen, where all
the machinery is hidden away. Shown here
is an 0-8-0 locomotive by Piko.

The HO gauge 2-6-2 TX 404, made of zamac by Liliput, is the copy of a locomotive built in 1919 by Jung.

*Specialist model train dealers are to be found all
over the world. Maybe in one of their windows
you will be fortunate enough to find such
treasures as this 0-10-0 B locomotive, by the
Austrian firm Roco, based in Salzburg.*

Another Austrian model, this Roco 2-10-0 C
would have specialized in transporting large loads.
It measures some 8.5 inches (21.3 cm) in length.

A 2-6-2 TB locomotive by Piko, a company that did business in the former East Germany from 1966 until 1990. Several versions of this model were produced, starting in 1967. Note the way the tender is integrated into the body of the locomotive. This model is a TB, in accordance with the chronological order in which the engines were designed, as there were already 2-6-2 TA locomotives in use.

*Another locomotive with integrated tender, this
2-6-2 TB was produced by Hornby for its acHO
collection, marketed in France. The original firm
founded by Frank Hornby stopped manufacturing
electric trains in 1963, although they were bought
out and so the Hornby name remains.*

The 0-8-0 D steam locomotive shown above, the brainchild of the engineer Garbe, was very successful—a total of over nine hundred of them are believed to have been produced. This Fleischmann model is made of plastic.

*A brass and bronze 0-6-0 TA Class produced
by RMA in the 1960s. The original dated
from 1867, when a total of 92 were built.*

*The prototype for this 2-10-0 Z locomotive
weighed just over 149 short tons (135 metric tonnes)
and had an 1625 hp engine. Its reference number
in the Fleischmann catalog is 4178, and it was
available in the colors of the various companies
who had used the original. To create the illusion
of steam billowing from the funnel, this model could
be fitted with the Seuthe number 9 smoke generator.*

This Liliput 2-10-0 Y is fitted with a light source that, in the dark, looks like a furiously stoked furnace. All it took to complete the illusion was a few drops of a special mixture (bought separately) in the funnel, and smoke would pour forth, just like a real steam train.

As you can see, this Jouef 2-10-0 X steam
locomotive has relatively small wheels. This is
because it did not need to go very fast as it was
primarily used to pull heavy loads.

*In Germany, this 4-6-2 locomotive with a
1625 hp engine was known as the Black Giant.
It was available in the Fleischmann catalog,
reference number 4170. Note the
characteristic smoke deflectors.*

In the colors of the Compagnie du Nord, this Pacific 4-6-2 was manufactured by Jouef and is made of plastic. For reasons of space, the tender is not pictured. The Compagnie du Nord colors, brown with highlights in gold, gives a certain touch of elegance. This model was first issued in 1977.

*This steam locomotive with the characteristic
rounded nose was first marketed by JEP in 1964.
It is a 4-6-4 SNCF, beautifully made of zamac,
of a an original dating from the early 1950s.*

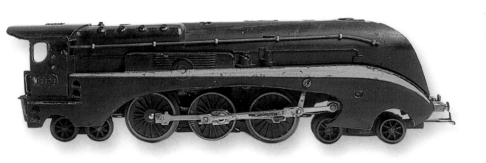

According to the great train specialist
Clive Lamming, this 4-6-4 TC was manufactured
from 1919 onwards by the Polish company Vulkan,
based in the town of Szczecin on the Oder river.
This is a plastic Liliput model.

The East German firm Piko enjoys a good reputation among model train enthusiasts. It produced this 2-10-0 Y steam locomotive. Note the magnificently detailed Heusinger connecting rods. This model was also equipped with a headlight for night journeys.

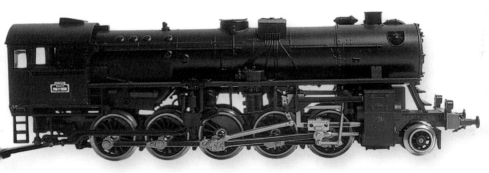

This Pacific 4-6-2 K in SNCF colors, measuring nearly 11 inches (27.7 cm), is a Jouef creation. The original was designed by the engineer Chabal, who, in 1909, worked for the French PLM rail company.

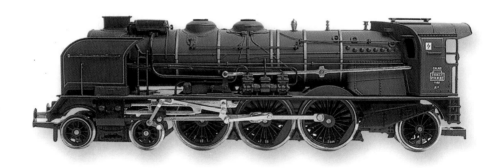

A superb 4-6-4 U steam locomotive and separate tender (not shown), built under the supervision of the engineer De Caso in 1949. It is known, and justly so, as La Divine. *This Jouef plastic model dates from 1980.*

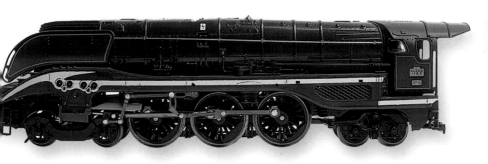

The 4-6-2 E 13 was designed by—and then named after—the engineer Chapelon. The model shown is by Rivarossi. The Compagnie du Nord ordered forty-eight of these 4-6-2 E series locomotives, starting in 1934.

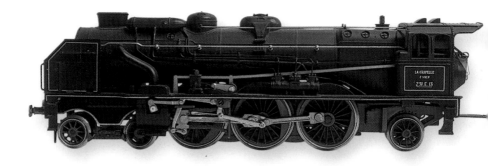

When it came out in February 1976, this 4-8-2 P7 Mountain, measuring 12.6 inches (32 cm), cost the princely sum of 176.70 francs. However, it was not the most costly item in the Jouef catalog—a 2-8-2 P Mikado went for nearly two hundred francs.

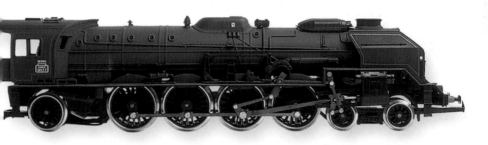

*The BB 66000 diesel locomotive had a top
speed of 75 miles (120 km) per hour, and
measured just over 49 feet (15 m) in length.
This model was produced by Jouef and
was sold from 1966 on.*

This BB 63000 diesel locomotive in SNCF colors was made by Roco in 1982. Like most of the HO scale locomotives in this chapter, it is made of plastic.

*Atop its original Jouef box, this is a BB 9200,
91 of which were built in the years after 1957. It would
have seen service on the south-eastern and south-
western rail networks in France.*

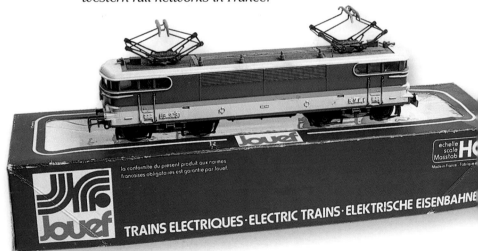

This HO scale model is Jouef's version of a
BB 17000 electric locomotive. The model represents
an engine with two rows of vents to help keep it
cool; early electric locomotives were functional but
not always elegant! Made of
plastic, it measures
just over 6.5 inches
(16.9 cm) in length.

Toys needn't be as expensive as the top-of-the-range models made by Märklin and other German manufacturers. Low-price plastic models can also prove of interest, for example this Fobbi version of a 1963 BB 67000 diesel locomotive, much in demand by collectors.

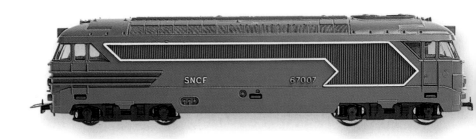

The Fobbi locomotive shown on the facing page is French; the firm Lima, which made the one shown below, is Italian. It is an SNCF CC 72000, built after 1968 by SACM-Alsthom.

Here we have a diesel shunter C 61000, dating from 1950. This model appeared in Jouef's 1979 catalog. In 1964, Jouef had already produced this engine's sister model, Y 51000, which measured a little over 4.5 inches (11.8 cm).

This is an SNCF DU 65 gang car, used for the upkeep of the rails, with a second car used for the tools and equipment. The two together were sold as reference 8525 in the Jouef catalog.

*This locomotive with an injection-molded plastic
body is an SNCF 2D2 5500, series 5538 to 5545.
The manufacturer is the French firm RMA,
which produced electric trains from 1951 to 1992.
Because of the rounded hoods at each end,
this engine was fondly compared to
a pregnant woman.*

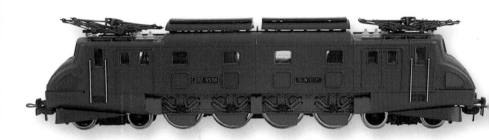

*Only one of the bogies is motorized on this HO scale
version of an SNCF 060 DB, some twenty of which
were built in the years after 1956. The plastic body
is extremely accurate in terms of detailing.
It is a Hornby acHO model.*

As is clear from the box shown on the facing page, Hornby used the first two letters of its name to establish a brand identity as a leader in H0 scale trains. The model shown below is an SNCF BB 12.061, designed by the engineer Nouvion. Between 1954 and 1961, 148 of them were built by the company MTE. The body of this model is in plastic, and the chassis is in zamac.

The CC 7121 is probably the crown jewel in Hornby's acHO collection. It is a copy of the locomotive that beat the world speed record in 1953 on a stretch of track between Dijon and Beaune in eastern France, attaining a top speed of nearly 152 miles (243 km) per hour.

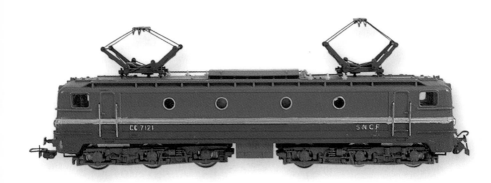

Here we have a basic JEP locomotive, not modeled on a particular engine, but characteristic of its time, when H0 had yet to dominate the model train market.

An X 3500 railcar, built by Renault, and given the name ABJ 3 Bigouden. In November 1928, when Raoul Dautry took charge of the French national rail network, it had only twelve electric railcars.

Like the railcar pictured above, this X 3600 Renault ABJ 4 was designed by the engineer Metzmaier. Both models are by AS. The ABJ 3 was produced by the Renault factory in 1939, and the ABJ 4 in 1948.

This Jouef X 4000 railcar is of the type
known as "Présidentiel," as the French
president frequently traveled on it.
It was designed and built
by Bugatti in its Molsheim
factory. Note the unusual
placing of the engineer, in the
middle with a lookout in either
direction! This vehicle had an
enormous impact on train design.

The X 4200 Panoramic, dating from 1959, had a top speed of about 81 miles (130 km) per hour. This is a Jouef model, made in 1966, and measuring just over 12 inches (30.5 cm) in length.

The firm De Dietrich began work on this X 42100 railcar in 1935. Four of them were built to order for the French rail company, Compagnie de l'Est. The example shown is an SNCF X 3700, built after the war, based on the pre-war X 42100 model. This model by AS has an electric motor, plastic body, and metal chassis.

This is a Standard Est X 23000 railcar, built by the company Aciéries du Nord in 1936. The original for this model measured 84 feet (25.55 meters) and weighed 51.8 short tons (47 metric tonnes). The model shown is by AS; it dates from 1983, and measures a little over 11 inches (just under 30 cm).

4509 frs 9.30

4505 frs 9.25

4508 frs 8.60

4504 frs 7.95

511 s 12.20

MÄRKLIN

4517 frs 15.90

4512 frs 22.50

IV

model trains
H0 SCALE CARS

A quick look at a few manufacturers' catalogs, a visit to a specialist model train dealer—that's all it takes to fall under the charm of the world of model train collecting. H0 scale trains, 1/87 real size running on rails 0.65 inch (16.5 mm) apart are the most popular now, because they are affordable, take up little space, and are the most readily available. However, they are not the smallest: Z scale trains are 1/220 real size, and run on rails a mere $1/4$ inch (6.5 mm) apart! Most collectors begin with H0 scale, and indeed, this scale has the largest range of locomotives and all sorts of cars: tank cars, cattle cars, baggage cars—a whole miniature world, just waiting to be discovered.

A French double-decker passenger car on four wheels. Such a car would have been a familiar sight on suburban routes. This plastic toy with its distinctive black-and-green body was produced by Jouef in 1969.

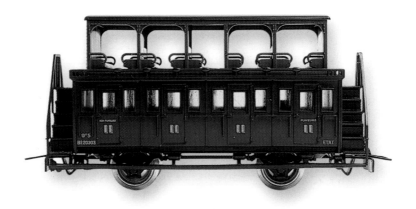

An old SNCF six-wheeled car with side doors and a brakeman's cab. This is a third-class C3 car as formerly used on the German network, the Deutsche Reichsbahn. The model shown is by Fleischmann, catalog reference number 8094.

This vehicle is a passenger car with a guard's compartment including room for some baggage, which saved having to use two different vehicles. Passengers would sit in the right half, and freight could be loaded in the left half. It is in tinplate, by JEP, catalog reference number 6652, and was manufactured from 1956.

This type of passenger car was described as a
"car with visible rivets," due to the large number
of molded rivets holding the metal sheets together.
Like the one on the facing page, this Jouef car
would have been divided into two parts,
for first and second class.

*A passenger car for a slow train, by Fleischmann.
The door is in the middle of the car, and just to the
right is the frosted glass window of the rest room.*

An SNCF BXE-type split-level suburban train. The model shown is by Jouef. The 1976 catalogue offers it for sale at 47.50 francs (reference number 5081). The first and second class cars for the same train (refs. 5082 and 5083) cost 41 francs.

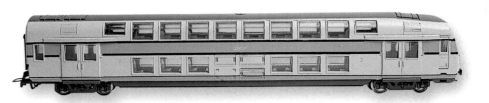

*Comfortably fitted-out inside and beautifully
proportioned, this car is a stainless steel A8
(the stainless-steel body is fabricated by the American
Budd method). The original was produced from 1952,
and more than four hundred were manufactured in
total for the French national train company SNCF.
The model shown is from the Hornby acHO collection.*

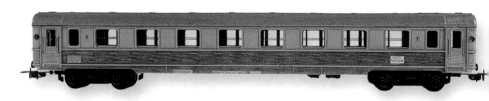

Many large companies, such as Agfa-Gevaert, would own their own freight cars or lease them on a long-term basis. Jouef made such cars in the colors of such well-known companies as Calberson, Spätenbräu, Findus, and, of course Jouef itself.

*For carrying loads such as this colourfully marked
moving company's road vehicle, special cars were
made with wheel wells to allow a standard trailer to
sit low enough to clear the railway loading gauge.
These single cars with a pocket for the wheels predate
the more modern long-welled vehicles in use today.*

Bailly was a company specializing in house moves from one continent to another. It had a huge fleet of trucks and containers which could fit on flatcars, either singly as on the facing page, or in twos, as in the Jouef model below.

This strange-looking car, sometimes known as a torpedo because of its shape, was used by the SNCF to transport molten cast iron for the company CAFL, based in the Loire region, south of Paris. This attractive model is by Lima, an Italian company. Like most model train manufacturers, Lima used a low-voltage direct current system (4 to 12 volts), the two rails being of different polarity.

Early diesel engines did not have the ability to
create steam to heat older steam-heated coaches,
so special cars were made with boilers.
This is a C922 boiler car, made by Jouef.
Such trains were used by the SNCF starting in 1960.

A freight car with the Coca-Cola logo.
All the manufacturers made versions of this car:
this one is by Piko.

Millions of tons of cereals were transported annually in hopper cars like this one. The car would be filled from the top and emptied at the bottom by the force of gravity. Algeco specialized in leasing out freight cars.

Some cars have two, three, or even more hoppers. This one, by Märklin, has five, and might have been used to transport, for example, aggregate. It is labeled as belonging to the German network, known as DB (Deutsche Bundesbahn) from 1948 until 1992.

Another type of car used in Germany for transporting aggregate, also made by Märklin. The hoppers can be removed from the base and tipped, making them very easy to load and unload.

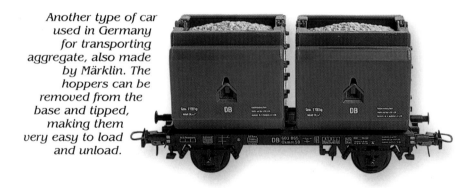

A very pretty tank car with separate axles by Jouef. It is in the colors of the Pierrefitte fertilizer company and is modeled on the OCEM tank first used in 1923. This model dates from 1965.

A cattle car by Liliput. Note the openwork sides allowing air to circulate freely. Surprisingly, this sort of car is rather unusual in HO scale modeling.

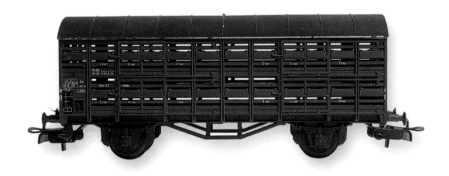

This delightful refrigerator car, of the sort used
by Interfrigo, is unusual in that the body is enclosed
in stamped cardboard. Refrigerator cars were used for
the transport of beer as early as 1867, when an
enterprising Austrian brewer sent a train full of beer
from Vienna to Paris. The model shown is by JL,
the company founded by Jean Lafont.

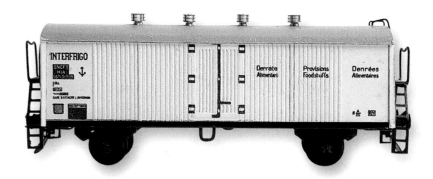

Tank cars have always been popular with manufacturers, children, and collectors alike. They were easy to produce, requiring only a single mold, after which the models could be given a multitude of logos.

*Engineers wrestled for a while with the problem
of how to transport products, such as asphalt, which
had to be kept hot. It would be loaded while hot,
and had to be maintained at this temperature for
hours or even days on end. This Shell insulated car
was made by Fleischmann.*

Jouef issued several car transporters, including this
STVA wagon, measuring nearly 6.8 inches (17 cm),
with room for six cars. Jouef also produced a larger,
more detailed, articulated model measuring 11.3 inches,
(28.6 cm) which could carry eight HO scale cars.

Crane cars have always
been popular because of the
level of technical detail they
offer in general, and also
simply because it is great
fun using the crane to
load and unload other
cars. The model
shown is by the
Austrian firm Roco.

Index,
Acknowlegments,
Addresses, and
Bibliography

Index

In this index you will find the main companies, brands, and models mentioned in this book.

TRAIN HORNBY

4-1E FABRIQUÉ PAR MECCANO-PT MADE IN FRANCE 4-1E

TRAIN HORNBY 4-1E "ÉTOILE DU NORD"

SNCF 1

2 SNC

INDEX

INDEX

INDEX

Alain Baldit is a real trai[
enthusiast. He runs th[
Rambolitrain museum i[
Rambouillet, south-wes[
of Paris in France[
which displays sever[
hundred model train[
(see following page[

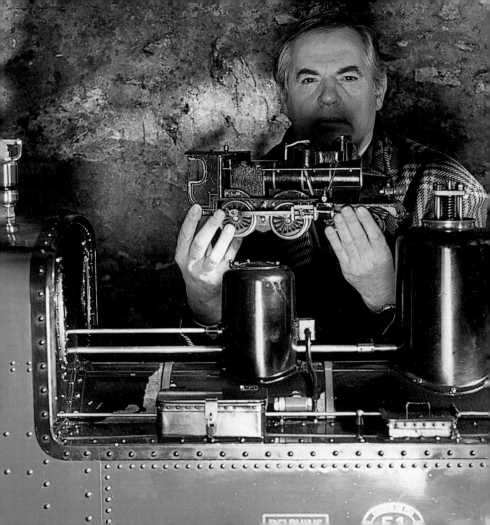

Acknowledgments and Addresses

*Two people who have been of great help with the task of photographing
and documenting this book are Alain Baldit and Guy Landgraf.
Alain Baldit is the curator of the Musée Rambolitrain.
4, place Jeanne d'Arc, 78120 Rambouillet, France
Tel.: +33 (0)1 34 83 15 93*

*Thanks are also due to Jean-Jacques Ehrlacher, maker of miniature trucks.
Tel.: +33 (0)1 30 88 50 46*

*And to François Binetruy, our permanent toy advisor.
Brocante de l'Orangerie, 33, rue de l'Orangerie, 78000 Versailles, France
Tel.: +33 (0)1 39 50 28 74 E-mail: fb78@wanadoo.fr*

*Thanks also to François-Xavier Sacase for his time and friendship;
and to Jean-François Krause who created the illustrations on pages 38 and 39.*

*Finally, grateful thanks to Andy McMillan from Countryside Models,
British designers and builders of model railways.
Tel.: +44 (0)1963 363544 www.countrysidemodels.co.uk*

For further advice and information contact:

*The Electric Train Company, 2 West Main Street, Victor, New York 14564
Tel.: (585) 924-1440 E-mail: sales@electrictraincompany.com*

The UK Model Shop Directory www.ukmodelshops.co.uk

North American Model Railroading Directory www.modelrailroads.net

Bibliography

Carlson, P. *Collecting Toy Trains*. London: New Cavendish, 1993.

Greenwald, D.E. *Easy Electronics Projects for Toy Trains*.
Milwaukee: Kalmbach Publishing, 1997.

Hollingsworth, S. *The Great Book of Trains*.
Minnesota: Motorbooks International, 2001.

Johnson, K. *Layout Plans for Toy Trains*.
Milwaukee: Kalmbach Publishing, 2001.

Rolt, L T C. *George and Robert Stephenson: The Railway Revolution*.
London: Penguin Books, 1960.

Sauter, G. *Modern Toy Trains*. Minnesota: Motorbooks International, 2002.

Schiphorst, P. K. *The Golden Years of Tin Toy Trains: 1850-1909*.
London: New Cavendish, 2002.

Stephan, E. A. *O'Briens's Collecting Toy Trains*. Iola: Krause, 1999.

Volhard, J. *Maintaining and Repairing your Scale Model Trains*.
Milwaukee: Kalmbach Publishing, 1999.

In the same collection

Collectible Wristwatches
by René Pannier
ISBN: 2-0801-0621-X

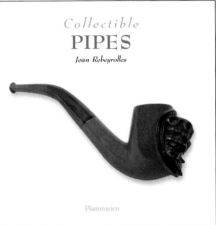

Collectible Pipes
by Jean Rebeyrolles
ISBN: 2-0801-0884-0

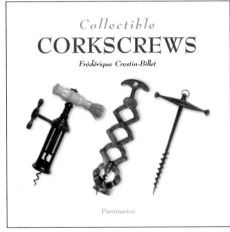

Collectible Corkscrews
by Frédérique Crestin–Billet
ISBN: 2-0801-0551-5

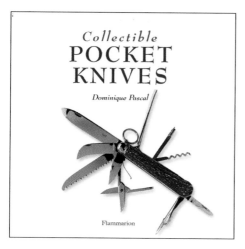

Collectible Pocket Knives
by Dominique Pascal
ISBN: 2-0801-0550-7

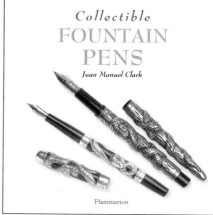

Collectible Fountain Pens
by Juan Manuel Clark
ISBN: 2-0801-0719-4

Collectible Miniature
Perfume Bottles
by Anne Breton
ISBN: 2-0801-0632-5

Collectible Lighters
by Juan Manuel Clark
ISBN: 2-0801-1133-7

Collectible Snowdomes
by Lélie Carnot
ISBN: 2-0801-0889-1

ISBN: 2-0801-0889-1

Collectible Playing Cards
by Frédérique Crestin-Billet
ISBN: 2-0801-1134-5

ISBN: 2-0801-1134-5

Collectible Miniature Cars
by Dominique Pascal
ISBN: 2-0801-0708-6

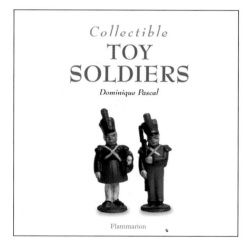

Collectible Toy Soldiers
by Dominique Pascal
ISBN: 2-0801-1141-8

Photographic credits